White Queen of the Cannibals: The Story of Mary Slessor

A. J. Bueltmann

CONTENTS

1

A Drunkard's Home

"On the west coast of Africa is the country of Nigeria. The chief city is Calabar, " said Mother Slessor. "It is a dark country because the light of the Gospel is not shining brightly there. Black people live there. Many of these are cannibals who eat other people. "

"They're bad people, aren't they, Mother? " asked little Susan.

"Yes, they are bad, because no one has told them about Jesus, the Saviour from sin, or showed them what is right and what is wrong. "

"Don't they have any missionaries out there, Mother? " asked blue-eyed Mary.

"Yes, there are a few and they are doing wonderful things for Jesus, but there are still thousands and thousands of people who have never heard a missionary. They need many, many more missionaries. "

"When I get to be a big man, I'm going to be a missionary, " said Robert, "and preach to the black people of Calabar and Nigeria. "

"I want to be a missionary; too, " cried Mary, tossing her red hair about.

"Girls can't be preachers, " said Robert.

"I want to preach to the black people, " said Mary, the tears racing down her cheeks.

"When I'm a missionary, " said Robert, "I'll take you into the pulpit with me. "

This made Mary happy and she was much happier when Mother Slessor said, "Perhaps you can be a teacher and teach the little black children of Calabar. Now, children, I want to be sure you know your memory verse for Sunday school tomorrow. Let's all say it together. " And Mother Slessor and her six children joined in saying:

Go ye into all the world and preach the gospel to every creature.

As they finished reciting the memory verse they heard a hoarse voice singing:

Gin a body-hic, meet a body-hic, Coming-hic, through the rye-hic.

"It's your father, children. Off to bed with you quickly now. Oh, I do hope Robert has brought some money home with him so that we can buy some food for tomorrow. "

"Where'sh the shteps? Somebody alwaysh moving the shteps, " said the father, Robert Slessor, as he staggered drunkenly to the door.

Mother Slessor took hold of him and led him to a chair.

"Hello, dear, " he said thickly. "Howsh my, besht gurl? There ish no shoemaker's got a prettier wife-hic-than I have. Yesh shir, we drank a li'l toash to you, my dear. "

"Oh, Robert, " said Mother Slessor to her husband, "I do hope you brought home some of your paycheck. We need it badly for food. We don't have any money in the house. All the food we have is what I kept back from the children's supper so you could eat. "

"Shure, I brought money home, " said Father Slessor. "All I did wash buy my friendsh a few drinksh. "

Mother Slessor's face brightened. At least they would be able to buy food. Her husband reached his hand into one pocket and brought it out empty. Then into another pocket and again brought it out empty. Finally trying several other pockets, he held out his hand with a small coin in it.

"Shee, there ya' are, I brought money home. There'sh a thrippence for ye. "

"Oh, Robert! " said Mother Slessor in dismay as the tears filled her eyes. "Oh, Robert! "

Then because she was used to these things, Mother Slessor heaved a sigh and said quietly, "Come and eat supper, Robert. "

The father staggered over to the table where Mrs. Slessor had placed the plate of food which the children had saved out of their own small helpings, that he might have something to eat.

"Who wants shupper? " said Father Slessor, and he threw the precious food into the fire. He staggered to his bed and fell into drunken sleep. With a deep sigh Mother Slessor put out the light and she, too, retired for the night. Early the next morning she was up, preparing breakfast. Carefully she scraped every bit of oatmeal out of the container and boiled it for breakfast.

"Come, children, it's time to get up. Sunday school this morning, " called Mrs. Slessor. Up jumped the six little Slessors. The older ones helped the smaller ones get dressed. When they had eaten the little oatmeal that Mrs. Slessor had for breakfast, they lined up for inspection.

"John, " declared Mrs. Slessor, "you did not wash behind your ears. Go with Mary and let her scrub the dirt away. Now I'll put a bit of perfume on your hankies, and here's a peppermint for each of you. There, off we go to Sunday school and church. "

Father Slessor snored in his drunken sleep, while the family went off to hear God's Word and to sing His praises. When they returned, Father Slessor was awake. He was sitting on the side of the bed and holding his head. He had "morning after" sickness.

"Come, Robert, " said Mrs. Slessor, "and sit up to the table. Good Elder McDougal has given us a bit of meat and some bread, so we can eat this day. "

Father Slessor groaned, but sat up to the table and ate dinner with his family. It wasn't much of a dinner. It would have been even less were it not for the kindness and charity of friends, because Father Slessor had spent all their money for drink.

After dinner the children did the dishes and ran out to play. When they were alone, Father Slessor hung his head and said,

"Oh, my dear, what can I say? I am so ashamed. I did so want to bring my wages home that we might have food for the children. And well—before I knew it, my wages were spent. "

"Robert, " said Mrs. Slessor, "you have said again and again that 'tis your friends who lead you astray. Would it not be well to move away to some other town where you can find new friends who will not drink and who will not tempt you to drink? "

"Aye, my dear, that no doubt would be the best. But where shall we go? "

"I have heard that there is plenty of work in Dundee, with the mills and all. Let's sell our things here and move to Dundee. "

"Aye, let us do that. 'Tis certain it won't be worse than here for you and the children. "

"Very well, then. I shall tell the children and we shall move before the week is out. "

When Mother Slessor went outside to call the children, she found Mary seated on the steps with her stick dolls about her.

"Well, Mary dear, what are you doing? "

"I am the teacher and these are the black children of Calabar. I am teaching them about Jesus. I am telling them that He saved them from their sins. "

Mother Slessor hugged her little teacher and told her about the move they planned to make. Then the other children were called and told, too. There was much excitement, especially when the furniture was sold and the Slessors with their remaining possessions took the train to Dundee.

It did not take long to find a place and get settled. Mother Slessor at once looked for a church they might attend. She found the Wishart

Church, named for the famous preacher, George Wishart, who in 1544 had preached near the place where the church was built. Shortly afterward he was killed for preaching about Jesus.

But Father Slessor did not do better in the new home. He could not overcome the drink habit, and probably did not try very hard to overcome it. In the meantime a new baby came to the Slessor home. They called the baby Janie. How happy her brothers and sisters were to welcome Janie! Mother Slessor was not altogether happy because she knew there was another mouth to feed. Father Slessor promised to give up drinking, but that did not mean anything, because he never kept those promises.

The money they got from selling their furniture in Aberdeen slowly melted away. Sickness came to the Slessor home. Robert Junior, who was going to be a missionary to Calabar, became sick and died. Two other of the children also died, and only Mary, Susan, John, and Janie were left. But even that did not make Father Slessor give up his drinking. The Slessors had less and less money to buy food. At last Mrs. Slessor went to work in one of the factories. Mary had to take care of the home. But the wages Mrs. Slessor received were very small. Somehow they had to find ways of getting more money. When she was eleven years old Mary went to work in the factory, too. Would she ever get a chance to be a missionary or must she give up that dream?

"Mary, Mary, " called Mrs. Slessor, "it's five o'clock. Time to get up and go to work. "

"Ho, hum, " said Mary, "I'm still tired, but I'll get right up. I don't want to be late! "

At six o'clock in the morning Mary was at work. She had to tend to the shuttles on the weaving machines. The weaving sheds where Mary worked were damp and dark. All morning long she heard the whirring of the belts and the clacking of the looms. In the afternoon she went to school. By the time she was fourteen years old she was an expert weaver. She now began to work full time.

The hours were long. Twelve hours every day for six days a week the fourteen-year-old girl worked in the factory. And the pay was very small. But it was a joy when she received her pay on Saturday night. Mary hurried home.

"Mother, Mother, " she called happily as she hurried into the house, "here is the money I earned this week. "

"Oh, Mary, that is so good of you, " said Mother Slessor. She wiped tears from her eyes with the end of her apron. She felt sad that Mary had to work in a factory. She thought of her own childhood in a happy home where there was always plenty to eat and plenty of money to buy things that were needed. She quickly hid Mary's wages in the same place where she hid her own wages, so that her husband would not find the money and spend it for drink.

Mary did not lose courage by the long hours in the factory. She remembered that David Livingstone, the great missionary, had worked in a weaving factory, too.

"If I want to be a missionary, I must study, " said Mary. "When can I find time? " Again Mary remembered something David Livingstone did when he was a boy. He would take books to work and read them when the weaving shuttles were working right and did not have to have someone attend to them. Mary did the same thing. She read many books from the Sunday school library. She read books like Milton's *Paradise Lost*. But most of all she read the Bible.

Conditions at home grew worse. Mary's drunken father became meaner and meaner. Saturday nights were the worst. Mary and her mother would sit waiting, after the younger children had been put to bed, for the father to stumble home. One night he was so mean to Mary, she had to run out of the house to get away from him. The whole family was unhappy because of Mr. Slessor's sinful habit. Finally, one morning he did not waken from the drunken sleep. In the night his soul fled to face the Judge in Heaven. The death of the father was really a great blessing to the family, for he had brought them only sorrow and trouble.

Now the family felt free. The load they had borne was lifted. Mary at once began to take a more active part in church work.

"If I want to be a missionary, I better have some practice. I know what I can do, I'll ask the Sunday school superintendent for a class to teach. " She did, and was given a class of girls. She enjoyed teaching the girls very much. She called them her "lovable lassies. "

But Mary was not satisfied. She wanted to get more practice.

On her way home from the factory Mary passed through the slums of the city. Mary herself did not live in a fine house; in fact, it was a very poor one. But in the slums the children lived in small, dark apartments. The streets on which they played were narrow and dirty. The children here did not know about the Saviour. They grew up rough and tough, cursing, swearing, stealing, and doing many mean things. Mary's heart ached for these children of the slums. She wanted to teach them that Jesus could make them happy. She talked with many people about it.

At last her church opened a mission in the worst part of the slums. Mary went to the superintendent.

"I want to teach a class in our mission, " said Mary. "I am sure you can use me better there than you can here. "

"But Mary, " said the superintendent, "you are doing a fine job here in the church; why do you want to go to the mission? "

"There are many who will gladly teach a class here at the church, but not so many who are willing to teach at the mission. I am willing. I will teach there if you will give me a class. Please do. "

"But Mary, those children are tough and mean. You couldn't handle them. You could not make them behave. You are hardly more than a child yourself. "

"Oh, please let me try, " said Mary, "I do so want to tell those boys and girls about my Saviour. Please let me try. Then if I don't make good, you can get someone else in my place. "

"Very well, " said the superintendent, "I will give you a class, but I warn you those children are tough and mean and hard to handle. "

2

A Brave Girl

"Quit pestering us to come to church. If you don't let us alone, we'll hurt you, " shouted Duncan, the leader of a group of tough boys in the slums.

Mary prayed God to make her brave and then said, "I will not stop trying to get you to come to church. I will not stop trying to tell you about Jesus, the Saviour. Do whatever you like. "

These boys had often tried to interrupt and break up the services, but Mary went out into the streets and tried to persuade and coax the young people to come and hear the Word of God.

"All right then, " said Duncan. "Here goes. " He took a piece of lead from his pocket and tied it to a long string. He began to swing it around his head. Each time he whirled the lead, it came closer to Mary's face. Mary did not move. The gang watched. They held their breath as it came closer and closer to her blue eyes. Mary did not blink. Finally, it grazed her forehead. Still Mary did not move. Duncan dropped the piece of lead to the ground.

"We can't scare her, boys, " he said. "She's game. "

"There is Someone who is far braver than I am. He's the One who makes me brave. Won't you come to the services and hear about Him? " asked Mary.

"All right, Spunky, I will, " said Duncan. "And the rest of the fellows will, too. Come on, boys, we're going to the church tonight and no funny business. "

This was not the only time that Mary had to face the tough boys and girls of the slums. But she had a Friend who was closer to her than even her dear mother. He made her strong and brave and true. Mary loved her Saviour, and was ready to do whatever He might want her to do.

Her class grew larger all the time. She visited the members in their slum homes. She fitted herself into the family. If the baby needed tending, she tended to it. If someone was sick, she helped to nurse the sick person. Always she told the family about Christ and His power to save. The people of the slums came to love this home missionary and many of them were won to Christ through her work.

The years went by. Did Mary still remember she wanted to be a missionary in Calabar? Yes, she remembered, but now she had all she could do to support her family. Since Robert, the would-be missionary, had died, Mother Slessor hoped that her youngest son John would be a missionary. But God had other plans. John became sick. He was sent to New Zealand for his health, but died when he arrived in that country. Was there to be no missionary from the Slessor family?

Whenever missionaries came to the Wishart Church or to Dundee, Mother Slessor, Mary, Susan and Janie would go to hear them. At home they would read the stories of missionaries and their work. They read missionary magazines. They read about the missionaries in China, Africa, Japan, India, and even Calabar.

One day William Anderson, a missionary to the West Coast of Africa, came to the little church. He told of the great need for missionaries in Africa. He told of the bad things which the people did who did not know Jesus.

Sitting in church, listening to the missionary, Mary saw in her mind a picture of Africa. It was not a beautiful picture. She saw captured Negroes being taken to other lands as slaves. She saw alligators and crocodiles swimming in the muddy waters, ever ready to eat black children who would come too close to the river. She saw cannibal chiefs at their terrible feasts and fearful battles with spears and arrows. She saw villages where trembling prisoners dipped their hands in boiling oil to test their guilt; where wives were killed to go with their dead chief into the spiritland. But these things did not frighten the Scottish girl who was afraid to cross a field if a cow was in it. She longed to go to Africa.

"Why don't I become a missionary? " Mary asked herself as she worked the looms in the factory. "Can I leave my home? Does Mother still need my help? Susan and Janie are working now. They could get along without me. But will I be brave enough? There are tropical jungles, and black men who eat people. There are wild animals, sicknesses, and death. God can make me brave to face all of these things. "

Mary prayed, "O God, if it is Your will, let me go as a missionary to Calabar. Let me be a teacher to teach these black people the story of salvation. You have commanded us, Your disciples, to carry the Gospel to the farthest parts of the earth. Use me, O Lord, to help carry it to Calabar. Hear me, for the sake of Jesus, my Saviour. "

It was 1874. The news flashed around the world: "Livingstone is dead. " The great missionary had died on his knees in Africa. Everywhere people were talking of this great man who had given his life to tell the people of Africa about the Saviour. Mary made up her mind! She must go to Calabar! But what would her mother say? And if her mother agreed, would her church send her out to that field? Mary went to her mother.

"I want to offer myself as a missionary, " said Mary Slessor to her mother. "Are you willing? "

"My child, I'll willingly let you go. You'll make a fine missionary, and I'm sure God will be with you. "

"Thank you, Mother, " said twenty-six-year-old Mary. "I know God will be with me and will make me strong and brave to serve Him. "

Mother Slessor was very happy. There was going to be a missionary in the family after all. But there were some people who did not agree with Mother Slessor. They shook their heads in doubt. Others thought Mary was very foolish to risk her life in that way.

"You're doing real well at the factory, " said one of them. "And you're doing missionary work right down there at the mission. Why rush away to those people way off in Africa? Seems to me missionary work ought to begin at home. "

"Yes, " said Mary, "it should begin there, but not end there. There are some who cannot go to Africa. They can do the work at home. If God lets me, I want to take His Word to those people who have never heard of Him or His love. "

The next year, 1875, Mary offered herself to the Foreign Mission Board of her church. She asked to be sent to Calabar. Then she waited. Waiting is hard sometimes. Mary had to wait until the Board had a meeting. Then when the meeting was over, she had to wait for the secretary of the Board of Foreign Missions to write her a letter. Early in 1876 the letter came. How excited Mary was! Her hands shook as she tried to open the letter. Had they accepted her offer or refused it?

"Mary dear, " said her mother, "you are so nervous, you had better let me open that letter. "

"I'll manage, Mother, " said Mary. She finally got it open, and she read:

Dear Miss Slessor, I take great pleasure in informing you that the Board of Foreign Missions accepts your offer to serve as a missionary, and you have been appointed teacher to Calabar. You will continue your studies for the teaching profession at Dundee. May God richly bless you in His service.

"Oh, Mother, I'm accepted! They're going to send me to Calabar! "

"Praise God from whom all blessings flow, " said Mother Slessor. "That is wonderful news indeed. To Calabar! Oh, I'm so happy I could shout for joy! "

In March another letter came. This letter told her that she was to spend three months at a teachers' college in Edinburgh. All Mary's friends in Dundee gathered at the train as she got ready to leave for Edinburgh.

"Come, Mary, " said Duncan, the tough boy from the slums, who was now a grown man and a faithful worker at the mission, "give us a speech. "

"I can't make a speech, " said Mary, "but I'll just ask you this: Pray for me. "

While Mary was at the school in Edinburgh, some of the other girls she met there tried to talk her out of being a missionary. They did not want her to go off to Africa where there were wild animals and man-eating heathen, and all kinds of terrible sicknesses.

"Don't you know that Calabar is the white man's grave? " asked one of her school friends.

"Yes, " answered Mary. "But it is also a post of honor. Since few volunteer for that section, I wish to go because my Master needs me there. "

At last the time had come for Mary to leave for Africa. For fourteen long years she had worked at the looms in the weaving factory. As she worked, she had dreamed of Calabar. Now her dream was going to come true. Mary went to the city of Liverpool. There she went on board the ship, the "S. S. Ethiopia. " As she got on board she looked around. Everywhere were barrels of whiskey.

"Hundreds of barrels of whiskey, but only one missionary, " said Mary sadly.

The boat whistle blew. The engines chugged. The "S. S. Ethiopia" was on its way. It was August 5, 1876. Mary saw the shoreline of Scotland become dimmer and dimmer. She looked forward to seeing the coast of Africa and the land of Calabar.

"At last I am on my way to Calabar, " said Mary Slessor as the "S. S. Ethiopia, " sailed southward. "How Mother would like to be with me! How often she prayed that God would send more missionaries to Calabar. I didn't think then that I would really be one of them. "

It did not take Mary long to make friends on board the ship. Among the friends she made were Mr. and Mrs. Thomson.

"So you are going to Calabar, " said Mr. Thomson. "Aren't you afraid of that wild country? "

"Oh, no, " said Mary, "because God is with me. He will take care of me. Jesus said, 'Lo, I am with you alway, even unto the end of the world, ' and I am trusting in His promise. "

"Do you know what this country is like? " asked Mrs. Thomson.

"Only what I have read about it, " said Mary. "You've been there before, haven't you? "

"Yes, we have, " said Mrs. Thomson. "My husband wants to build a home where tired missionaries can rest and rebuild their strength for their wonderful work. He has explored the West Coast and chosen the Cameroon Mountains as the place for that home. We are going there now to build this home for missionaries. Missionary work in Africa is so hard that missionaries need a place where they can rest from time to time. "

"I think that's wonderful of you! " said Mary. "I know the Lord will bless the work you are doing. Won't you tell me about Africa? "

"Well, " said Mr. Thomson, "the climate is very hot. The sun is so strong and hot that white people don't dare go out without a hat to protect their heads. The rivers are very muddy and often flow through dark, gloomy swamps that white people can hardly get through. "

"But often, " broke in Mrs. Thomson, "there are beautiful green banks with the most beautiful flowers. You will see the prettiest birds in all the world dressed in the brightest reds and greens and blues and purples. You will see the long-legged cranes and the funny pelicans with their big beaks. "

"And don't forget the man-eating crocodiles that are swimming in the river or lying on the banks. They look like an old log, but if you get near them, look out! They seem lazy and slow, but they can snap off a leg or drag you into the river as quick as a wink. Then in the jungles are the lions, and elephants, and other wild animals. "

"I am most frightened of the swift and terrible tornadoes, " said Mrs. Thomson.

"And, Miss Slessor, " said Mr. Thomson, "don't forget that the natives are wild and fierce and many of them are cannibals who would be glad to eat you. "

"I shall not fear, " said Mary. "God is leading me. He is my good Shepherd. He can protect me from fierce beasts and the wild people. I am happy He has chosen me to bring the messages of the Saviour to these wild people. He will call me home to Him when the work He has for me is done. Till then nothing can really harm me. "

Four weeks passed. The ship was plowing through the tropical sea. The air was warm, but the sea breezes made it very pleasant. The ship turned landward and soon Mary could see the shore of Africa. How thrilled and happy she was—Africa at last! On September 11 the ship entered the tumbling, whirling waters of the Cross and Calabar Rivers which here joined and poured into the sea. Mary had read about these rivers, and now she actually saw them. She saw, too, the pelicans and the cranes. She saw crocodiles, about which Mr. Thomson had told her, lazily slide off the sandbanks into the muddy waters of the river.

Mr. and Mrs. Thomson stood with Mary at the rail of the ship as it sailed up the river. They would point out to her interesting sights as they passed along.

"Look, " said Mrs. Thomson, "there is Duke Town. That is where your mission is. "

Mary saw clay cliffs. She saw mud houses with roofs of palm leaves. Duke Town did not look in the least like Dundee or the other cities in Scotland which Mary knew. Duke Town did not look pretty, but Mary did not care. To her it looked beautiful, because here she would have the chance to serve the Lord.

Soon native canoes came out to the steamer. Then the boats of the traders. All was hurry and bustle as the great ship anchored and prepared to unload the part of its cargo that had been sent to Duke Town. Mary looked about, wondering how she was going to go ashore.

A tall Negro came up to Mary. He bowed and said, "Are you the new white ma that is coming to the mission? " By ma the native meant lady. They called all white ladies "ma. "

"Yes, I am, " said Mary.

"Mr. Anderson sent me to bring you ashore and take you to the mission house. "

14

Mary was lowered from the great ship into a large canoe. Her baggage was brought down and placed in the boat. Then with powerful strokes the rowers sent the boat skimming across the water toward Duke Town. Mary was helped ashore by the tall Negro who had come for her.

"At last, " she said to herself, "at last I am in Calabar. "

3

In Africa

"Welcome, welcome, Mary, " said "Mammy" Anderson, as she hugged Mary. Mammy Anderson and her husband, William Anderson, were among the first missionaries at Duke Town in Calabar. "This is Daddy Anderson, " said Mammy Anderson, "and Daddy, this is Mary Slessor, just come from bonny Scotland to help us. "

Daddy and Mary shook hands. "Long ago you preached in our church in Dundee, " said Mary. "You told how many missionaries were needed. I wished then I could help you. I hope I can. "

Mary liked this fine Christian couple from the start. The mission house where they lived was high on a hill above the town. Mammy took Mary around the house and the yard, which they called a compound. She showed Mary where the workers stayed who helped at the mission house. She showed her the school where the little black children were taught to read and write and told of the dear Saviour who had died for them, too, that they might be saved from sin and Hell and go to Heaven.

"And here, " said Mammy, "is the bell. I am putting you right to work. One of your jobs will be to ring the rising bell for morning prayers. You ring this at six o'clock. Then everyone will get up, and we will have prayers in the chapel. "

That was Mary's first job, but alas! Mary often overslept and did not ring the rising bell in time. One morning she awoke and saw that it was very bright outside.

"Dear me, " said Mary, "I've overslept again. " She jumped out of bed, slipped into her clothes and rang the bell, loud and long. Soon the workers began coming, rubbing their eyes and yawning.

"What's the idea of ringing the bell now? " asked one of them. "It's much too early. "

"But look how bright it is, " said Mary.

16

Daddy Anderson laughed.

"Mary, Mary, " he said, "it's only two o'clock in the morning. The light you see is our bright tropical moon. It's not the sun. " And all the workers laughed, and Mary laughed with them.

"I guess I'm not a very good bell-ringer, " she said.

Mary's real job was to teach the children in the school on Mission Hill. She remembered how she had played when she was a little girl that she was teaching the children of Calabar. Now she was really doing it. She loved the little black children. After school she would take long walks with them into the bush. There they saw beautiful birds of many bright colors, and beautiful flowers of all kinds.

Mary ran races with the black children. How they loved that! She climbed trees as fast as any boy. The black children loved their white ma who taught them and played with them. But playing with the children often made Mary late for meals.

"Mary, Mary, " scolded Mammy Anderson gently, "you are late again. I am going to punish you. You go to your room. Since supper is over, you'll just have to go to bed without it. "

Mary went to her room. In a little while she heard a knock at her door.

"It's Daddy, Mary, " said a deep voice. "Please open your door. "

Mary opened the door. There stood Daddy Anderson with his hands full of biscuits and bananas which he was bringing to her with Mammy's consent.

"I thought you might be hungry, " said Daddy Anderson.

"You and Mammy are perfect dears, " said Mary. "I don't deserve all your kindness. " Mary soon began to visit the different yards or compounds in Duke Town. Missionaries had been here for thirty years, but there weren't many of them. They worked chiefly in Duke Town, Old Town, and Creek Town—three towns at the mouth of the Calabar River. They also had opened a station at Ikunetu and Ikorofiong on the Cross River. One day Mary was at one of the stations with another missionary. When he finished his talk, he said, "Mary, won't you speak to these people? "

Mary stood up. "Please read John 3:1-21, " she said. The missionary did. Then Mary told the people how they could be born again. She told them of the joy that they would have if they took Jesus into their hearts. She told them of the hope of life after death with God in Heaven. The natives listened. They liked her talk. After that whenever she came to that district, crowds would come to hear her speak.

"Mammy, " said Mary, after she had come from a trip to the outstations, "it hurts my heart to see how cruel these people are. And those awful, ugly, cruel gods they pray to. The chiefs are so cruel and mean and have no mercy. And then that terrible secret society, the Egbo. I saw some of their runners dressed in fearful costumes scaring the people and whipping them with long whips. I saw a poor man whom they had beaten almost to death. Then there is that horrible drinking. They are worse than wild animals when they become drunk. And worst of all is that they have slaves and sell their own people as slaves. "

"Ah, lassie, " said Mammy Anderson, "you haven't seen anything yet. There are millions of these black people in the bush and far back in the interior. Most of them are slaves. They don't treat a slave any better than a pig. The slaves sleep on the ground like animals. They are branded with a hot iron just as animals are. And just as the farmers back home fatten a pig for market, so the girls are fattened and sold for slave wives. The slaves can be whipped or sold or killed. When a chief dies, the tribe cuts off the heads of his wives and slaves and they are buried with him. The tribes are wild and cruel. Many of them are cannibals, who eat people. They spend their lives in fighting, dancing, and drinking. But the way they treat twins is one of the worst things they do. "

"What do they do to twins? " asked Mary.

"They kill them, " said Mammy Anderson. "Sometimes they bury the twins alive and sometimes they just throw them out into the bush to die of hunger. The mother is driven into the bush. No one will have anything to do with her. She is left to die in the jungle or to be eaten by the wild animals. "

"But why do they do such cruel, wicked things to harmless babies? " asked Mary.

"They believe that the father of one of the twins is an evil spirit or devil. But they don't know which one's father was a devil, so they kill both to be sure of getting the right one. "

"That must be stopped, " said Mary. "I will fight it as long as I live. I will never give up. Jesus loves twins just as much as other children. The natives must learn that. They must learn that God said, 'Thou shalt not kill. ' I'll teach them. "

Mary made many friends, not only among the children whom she taught, but also among the grown-up natives. One day she heard a chief speaking to his people about God and His love. He was a Christian. Mary thought that he made a very fine talk. She could tell he was very sincere. He talked so that everyone could understand him.

"Who is that chief? " asked Mary of the man standing next to her.

"That is King Eyo Honesty VII, " said the man.

"King Eyo Honesty? I must talk to him. "

As soon as she could, Mary went up to the chief.

"King Eyo Honesty, " said Mary, "I am Mary Slessor. Many years ago the missionaries told my mother about you. They told her what a fine Christian you were. She told us. She will be very happy when I tell her that I have met you. "

"I am very happy to have met you, " said King Eyo Honesty. "Perhaps I could write a letter to your mother and tell her how happy I am that I have met you. I would tell her how happy I am that her daughter has come to teach my people about God. "

"Mother would be very happy, I know, to get a letter from you. "

For many years the African chief and Mary's Scottish mother wrote letters to one another.

Every day when school was over, Mary went to visit the natives in their homes. She would tell them about Jesus and how He loved them. She told them Jesus wanted to save them. She told them that Jesus had paid for their sins by dying for them. If they loved and trusted in Jesus, He would take their sins away.

One Sunday morning as she was walking through the village, she saw one of the old men who came to church all the time sitting at the door of his mud house. He looked very sad.

"Ekpo, " said Mary, "why aren't you on your way to God's house? Mr. Anderson will be looking for you. He will miss you. "

"If your heart were sad, would you go any place? " asked Ekpo.

"But why is your heart sad? "

"My son, my only son, is dead. Even now he is buried in the house. "

"Ekpo, let me tell you a story, " said Mary. "A long time ago there were two sisters. They had a brother. They loved him very much. They loved him like you loved your son. He became sick. The two sisters sent a messenger to Jesus to tell Him. When Jesus came, the brother was dead. Martha, the one sister, said to Jesus, 'Lord, if You had been here my brother would not have died. I know that even now God will give You whatever You ask Him. '

"Jesus said, 'Your brother will get up from the grave. '

"Martha said, 'I know that he will get up from the grave in the resurrection at the last day when all the dead shall come out of their graves. '

"Jesus said to her, 'I am the resurrection and the life. He who believes in me, even though he dies, he will live. Whoever lives and believes in me shall never die. '"

"Did the brother get up from the grave? "

"Yes, Jesus went to the grave and said, 'Lazarus, come out, ' and Lazarus did. But, Ekpo, later Lazarus died again. Then his body stayed in the grave, but his soul was with God. He was happy. All Christians are happy with God. Your son was a Christian, wasn't he?"

"Oh, yes, Ma, he was, " said Ekpo's wife, who had come to the door while Mary was talking.

"Then don't you see, God has taken him. He is with God. He is happy. If you believe in Jesus, then some day you, too, will be with God and will see your son again. "

"Well, " said Ekpo, "if God has taken him, it is not so bad. "

"Come, then, " said Mary, "let's go to God's house and thank Him that your son was a Christian and is now with God in Heaven. "

Mary knew there was a great deal to do. There were so many people who did not know about Jesus. There were so many who were terribly mean and cruel. But Mary knew that with the Lord on her side she would not lose in the fight against sin and wickedness. Every day she would tell the natives about Jesus. Every day she would show them their sins and the Saviour.

For three years Mary worked hard. Then she became sick. It was the terrible coast fever. Sometimes she was so sick, she did not know what was happening. She was very tired. She wished that she could see her mother and sisters.

"Calabar needs a brave heart and a strong body, " said Mary. "I don't have much of a brave heart, but I often feel the need of it when I am sick and lonely. "

"Mary, you must go home to Scotland and rest, " said Mammy Anderson, "then you will get well from the fever. You will never get well here. "

"That's true, Mammy, " said Mary, "but you know that I cannot leave my field of work was until the Board of Missions says I may. "

"That's right, but you have a furlough coming. I do hope we hear from the Board soon. "

In June, 1879, the letter came. Mary read it gladly. It told her that she could come home for a year's vacation. It did not take Mary long to pack. She left for Scotland on the next steamer. There were tears in her eyes as she stood on the deck. There on the shore were her black friends waving good-by to their white ma. They were crying, too.

"Come back again! Come back again! God bless you and keep you! " they said.

Mary waved to them.

"I will be back, " she said. Mary loved Africa. She loved the people there, but she knew if she wanted to get well she would have to go home. Then, too, she was anxious to see her mother and sisters again.

The ocean trip did Mary much good. The cool ocean breezes blew the fever away. It made her cheeks pink again. Every day she prayed for the people of Africa. She prayed that she might go back again. She prayed that more missionaries would be sent out to show these poor people the way to Heaven.

How happy Mary's mother and two sisters were to have her with them again! And how happy Mary was to be with them! They could not hear enough about Calabar. It made Mary's mother very happy to know that her daughter had taught the black children the way to Heaven. She was glad to hear about the other missionary work which Mary had done. But other people, too, were anxious to hear about Calabar. So Mary had to speak at Wishart Church and other churches.

Mary told about the heathen, the wicked things the heathen natives did to twins, the mean way they treated slaves, and the many other cruel, wicked things these people did.

"There is only one thing that will change these people, " said Mary. "There is only one thing that will turn these heathen from their sins. That is the Gospel of Jesus Christ, the good news about the Saviour. But who will tell these people about Jesus? We need many, many more missionaries. If you cannot go yourself, you can send gifts and offerings for this work. We need money so the missionaries can buy food and clothing. We need money so that they can build homes and churches and hospitals. Have pity on these poor people! Pity the poor little children! Help them now! Above all, pray for these people, and pray for your missionaries that God will bless their work with these lost souls. "

Everywhere Mary went she won friends for Calabar. The people who heard Mary wanted to help make Christians of the heathen people. Many prayed. Many gave. Men and women gave gifts of money for the work. Boys and girls brought their little gifts, too. They knew the hymn:

If you cannot give your thousands You can give the widow's mite. And each gift you give for Jesus Will be precious in His sight.

Mrs. Slessor was not well. Living in the crowded, dusty, smoky city made her sick. Mary found a little home out in the country. Here were clear blue skies and pleasant fields. Mary's mother was much better after they moved her. Mary's sisters enjoyed it also. The months passed quickly. Soon the year would be over.

"What do you want to do when you go back? " asked Mrs. Slessor.

"I want to go on up the river. I want to go where missionaries have never been. I want to go to Okoyong and tell the people there about Jesus. I am praying God that sooner or later He will let me go and work there. "

"Isn't it much more dangerous there? " asked Mrs. Slessor.

"Yes, it is, " answered Mary, "but I am not afraid because I know that God is with me and His angels are watching over me. "

June came. Mary had been home a year. Now she was in good health again. She wanted to get back to Africa. July, August, September went by and then the good news came. Mary was to leave in October for Calabar. It was a happy day for her when she got on the ship that would take her back to the Africa she loved.

On the ship she found the Rev. and Mrs. Hugh Goldie. They, too, had been missionaries in Calabar for many years, and now after a short vacation were going back once more. All the way to Africa the friend talked about the great work of winning souls for Jesus, especially the souls of the people of Calabar.

At last the big steamship entered the mouth of the Calabar and Cross Rivers. It was not far now to Duke Town. Soon Mary would learn what work she should do. Would it be work she wanted to do? Would it be work in the jungles? Mary would soon know.

4

On Her Own

"Mary, how would you like to have a mission station of your own? " asked Daddy Anderson.

"Why, I'd love it, " answered Mary.

"It is hard work and very unpleasant at times, " said Daddy Anderson.

"I don't care how hard or unpleasant it is, " said Mary, "as long as I can work for my Lord. "

"Good, then you will be in charge of the Old Town Station, two miles up the river. "

It did not take Mary long to pack her things and move to Old Town. But what a sight greeted her when she arrived! The first thing she saw as she came into the village was a man's skull hanging from the end of a pole and swinging slowly in the breeze.

"Where is the mission house? " asked Mary of one of the natives.

"Down that way at the end of the road, Ma, " he answered.

Mary found the mission house. It was an old tumble-down shack. It was made of long twigs and branches, daubed over with mud. The roof was made of palm leaves. It was not nearly as nice a home as the one on Mission Hill in Duke Town. When Mary went inside, she found that it was whitewashed and somewhat clean. Mary got busy cleaning up her house, and as she did, she began to make her plans.

"I don't care if my house is not so fine. I am nearer to the jungles. I want to get into the jungles sometime and win those poor, ignorant heathen people for Jesus. I am going to live in a house like the natives and use the tools and things they do—only I'll be a lot cleaner. Then they will feel that I am one of them and I'll be better able to win them for Jesus. Then, too, it's cheaper to live that way and to eat bananas. I will be able to send more money home to my poor mother in Scotland. Living this way will also help me get ready for the time when I can go into the jungles. Then I will have to live that way. "

Mary held services every Sunday. She started a day school for the children. The grownups came, too. Mary was so friendly and kind that the natives loved her. More and more came to hear about Jesus. Mary showed them that He was the Saviour of the blacks and whites alike. Many came from faraway places to hear the white ma and go to her school.

Mary soon visited all the villages in the neighborhood and every place she went she would tell the people about Jesus. At one place the king of that part of the country came regularly to hear the white ma. He would sit on the bench with the little children and listen to Mary tell about the Saviour who loves all people.

One thing still bothered Mary very much. This was the way the natives treated twins. As soon as twins were born, they would break the babies' backs and stuff the little bodies into a jar made out of a big gourd. Then they would throw the jar out into the jungle. The mother would be sent away out into the jungle to die.

"It is very wicked for you to kill these twin babies, " said Mary to the people. "It is a sin against God, who said, 'You shall not kill people. ' Jesus loves all children. He loves the twin babies, too. "

The natives would not listen to her. They were afraid of the evil spirits. One day Mary heard about some twins that were born. She rushed over to the house and took the babies before they were killed. She brought them to her house and took care of them.

"She will have lots of trouble taking an evil spirit into her house, " said one of the natives. "Just you wait and see. "

"Maybe she is a friend of the evil spirit, " said another.

But weeks and months went by and nothing happened. The people began to see that Mary was right. Everywhere the people began to call Mary "the white ma who loves babies. "

Another wicked thing the people did was to kill the babies of slaves who died. They did not want to bother taking care of them so they killed them. Mary began to take these little orphans into her home and take care of them. But it began to be too much work for Mary alone. She wrote a letter to the Mission Board asking for someone to take care of these children.

One day a trader came and knocked at Mary's door. He was carrying a little black baby in his arms.

"I found this twin out in the bush, " said the trader. "The other one was killed. This baby would have died, but I know how you love these little ones, so I brought it to you. "

"Thank you, " said Mary, taking the tiny baby in her arms. "I shall call her Janie, after my sister. " Mary adopted the little baby and the baby brought Mary much joy and happiness.

One time Mary took a baby six months old into the mountains. The baby was sick. In the valley it was very hot.

"This child shall not die if the cold can save him, " said Mary.

Up in the mountains it was much cooler than in the valley. Mary pitched her tent and stayed there for a time so the baby could get well.

One night Mary woke up. She heard a growling noise. She looked around. A panther was in the tent! He had the baby in his mouth! He was going to carry it away!

Mary jumped up. She grabbed a burning stick from the fire and rammed it into the panther's face. With a wild howl the panther dropped the baby and ran off. Mary picked up the baby who was crying now. She looked him over, carefully. He was not hurt. Softly she sang to the baby and rocked him to sleep. After the baby was well, Mary went back to the mission station in the valley.

Another time news came that twins had been born. All the people had thought a lot of the mother, even though she was a slave. Now everyone hated her. The other women in the house cursed her. They broke up the few dishes she owned. They tore up her clothes. They would have killed her but they were afraid of Mary Slessor and what she would do.

They took the two babies and stuffed them into an empty gin box and shoved it at the woman.

"Get out! Get out! " they said, "you have married the Devil. You have a devil in you. " They threw rocks at her and drove her out of the village.

Mary met the poor woman carrying her babies in the box on her head. The screaming, howling crowd of people were following her.

"Go back! Go back to your village, " Mary told the crowd. Then turning to the woman she said, "Give me the box and come with me to my house. "

When Mary opened the box, she found one child dead. The baby's head had been smashed when it was jammed into the box. Mary buried the poor little baby. Soon the owner of the woman came and took her back. She was willing to do this as long as she had no children. The little baby stayed with Mary and became another of her family.

One evening Mary was sitting on the porch of her mission house talking to the children. Suddenly they heard a loud noise. They heard the beating of drums. Then they heard men singing loudly.

"What's that? " asked Mary. She took the twin boys that were with her and rushed down to the road to see what was going on. Here she found a crowd of people. They were all dressed up. Some wore three-cornered hats with long feathers hanging down. Some had crowns. Some wore masks with animal heads and horns. Some put on uniforms with gold and silver lace. Some just covered their bodies with beadwork and tablecloths trimmed with gold and silver.

When Mary came, the shouting stopped. The king came forward to meet her.

"Ma, " said the king, "we have had a palaver. We have made new laws. The old laws were not God's laws. Now all twins and their mothers can live in town. If anyone kills twin babies or hurts the mothers, he shall be hung. "

"God will bless you for making those wise laws, " said Mary.

The mothers of the twins who lived at the mission and other mothers, too, gathered around Mary. They laughed and shouted. They clapped their hands, and with tears running down their cheeks, cried: "Thank you! Thank you! " They made so much noise that Mary asked the chief to stop them.

"Ma, how can I stop these women's mouths? " asked the chief. "How can I do it? They be women. "

Mary was happy, but after a while some of the people began to forget the new laws. Quietly and underhandedly they began to go back to doing the old bad things again. This was because they were not Christians. They did not love and trust the Saviour. Mary knew that the main thing to do if she were to get them to live right and do right was to change their hearts. New laws could not really change them. Only faith in Jesus could do that.

"I must help them more. I must lead more of them to Jesus, " said Mary. "Many are sick. I will give them medicine, and at the same time tell them about Jesus who makes the soul well and the body, too. "

As Mary gave out medicine, many people would often crowd around her to hear her "Jesus talk. " She told them of Jesus' love for them. She told them how He had died that they might be saved from everlasting death and be made pure. Mary had her hardships. Often she would not be able to get home at night and would have to sleep in the open. It was not easy to be a missionary, but Mary was gladly willing to do it because she was working for Jesus and saving souls.

One day a man came to the mission house.

"I am the servant of King Okon. King Okon has heard of the white Ma. King Okon has heard how the white Ma loves our people and is kind to them. King Okon invites the white Ma to come and visit our country. "

"I shall be glad to come if I may tell your people about Jesus, the Saviour, " said Mary.

"Sure, " said the messenger, "you come and make Jesus-talk. "

When King Eyo Honesty VII, Mary's old friend, heard of this invitation, he said:

"Our Ma must not go as an ordinary traveler to this savage land and people. She must go as a lady and our mother, one whom we greatly respect and love. "

He brought his own canoe to Mary and said, "The canoe is yours to use as long as you wish. "

Mary's eyes filled with tears of thankfulness.

"King Eyo, " she said, "I thank you from the bottom of my heart. I accept the offer of your canoe in Jesus' name. I know God will bless you for your kindness. "

"God has blessed me, " said the king. "He has sent our white Ma to us. "

The canoe was long and slim. It was painted in bright colors. At the front end bright-colored flags were flying. In the middle of the canoe was a sort of tent to protect Mary from the sun. The Christian natives had brought gifts of rice and these were put in the boat. Crowds of people came to say good-by to the white Ma. At last it began to get dark. The thirty-three natives who were going to row climbed into the boat. Torches were lit and the boat started upstream.

As Mary lay down in her tent in the middle of the boat, she heard the rowers singing as they rowed.

"Ma, our beautiful beloved mother, is on board, " they sang, "Ho! Ho! Ho! "

She thanked God that He had protected her in Old Town. She prayed that He would protect her still as she went into a part of the country where no one had yet brought the news about a loving

Saviour. She prayed that He would bless her speaking, so that many people would believe in the Lord Jesus and be saved forever.

As she prayed, the rowers continued singing their made-up song: "Ma, our beautiful beloved mother, is on board. Ho! Ho! Ho! "

Mary fell asleep and the canoe carried her silently through the night to a new part of the country and to new adventures.

When the sun arose the following morning, the canoe carrying Mary Slessor arrived at King Okon's village. A great shout went up from the people when they heard the white Ma had come.

"You have my room, " said the chief. "It is the best room in the village. "

It may have been the best room, but it was not a very comfortable one. Rats and big lizards were running back and forth across the floor. There were insects and fleas and lice everywhere.

The people were much interested in the white Ma. They had never seen a white woman before. They crowded into the yard. Many of them touched and pinched Mary to see if she were real. Some were afraid. Their friends laughed at them and pulled them into the yard. They watched Mary eat. They watched everything she did. Mary did not care. She used their interest in her to tell them about Jesus who loved them. She told them that they must love Jesus and trust in Him for salvation.

Twice a day she held services and great crowds came to hear her. She cut out clothes for the people and taught the women how to sew. She gave medicine to the sick and bandaged the wounds of those who got hurt.

"King Okon, " said Mary, "I would like to go into the people's homes in the jungle. May I go? "

"No, white Ma, I cannot let you go. This is elephant country. The elephants go wild and run over everything in the jungle. These stampedes have been so bad my people have had to leave off farming and make their living by fishing. I cannot let you go. You might get hurt or killed. "

One night Mary saw that the people looked very angry. Some were sad.

"What is the matter? " asked Mary.

"Two of the king's young wives have done wrong. They have broken a law, " answered one of the natives. "They thought nobody was looking and went into a room where a young man was sleeping. Each of them will be hit a hundred times with a whip. "

Mary went to the king. She asked him to be kinder to these girls. She begged him not to beat them so much.

"Ma, you are right, " said the king. "I will call palaver of all the chiefs. If you say we must not whip girl, we must listen to you as our guest and Ma. But the people will say God's Word be no good, if it keeps the law from punishing those who do wrong. "

Mary saw the king was right. She turned to the girl-wives of the king.

"You have brought shame to the king and the tribe by the silly foolish things you did. God's Word teaches men to be kind and merciful and generous, but it does not pass over sin or permit it. I cannot ask the king not to punish you. Ask God to help you in the future, so that you will not do bad or foolish things. "

All the chief men of the tribe grunted their approval of what Mary had said to the girls. But then Mary turned to the chief men and said:

"You are to blame. Your custom of one man marrying many wives is wrong and cruel. These girls are only sixteen years old and still love fun and play. They are too young to be married. They meant no real harm. "

The men did not like to hear that. They did not like to hear that their ways were wrong.

"If punishment is hard, " said the old men, "wife and slave will be afraid to disobey. "

"King Okon, " said Mary, "show that you are a good king by being kind and merciful. Don't be too hard on these young girls. "

"All right, Ma, " said the king, "I will make it only ten blows with the whip. Also we will not rub salt into the wounds to make them sting. "

When the whipping was over, Mary took the girls into her room. There she put healing medicine on their backs while she told them about Jesus who could heal their souls.

At last it was time for Mary to go back to Old Town. The king and the people were sorry to see her go. On her homeward way a tropical storm struck the canoe and the people in it. Mary was soaked. The next morning she was shaking with sickness and fever. The rowers feared their white Ma would die. They rowed as fast as they could for Old Town. Mary was so sick that she had to take a long rest.

A few months later a big storm tore off the roof of her house and again she was soaked as she worked to save the children. Again she became very sick.

"You must go home to Scotland, " said Daddy Anderson. "You must go home and rest and get well. "

"Since you tell me to do that and the Board has ordered it, too, I can only obey, " said Mary. "I am going to take my little black Janie with me. It is too dangerous to leave her here where some of the heathen might steal her and kill her because she is a twin. "

With a heart that was sad at leaving Calabar, but glad to have a chance to see her dear ones in Scotland again, Mary sailed for Dundee in April, 1883.

5

Into the Jungle

"Oh, Mary, it is good to see you again, " said Mother Slessor when Mary arrived once more in Scotland. "And this is little Janie about whom you have written us so often! We are happy to have you with us, Janie. "

"I am glad to be home, Mother, " said Mary, "but I am anxious to go back to Africa as soon as I can. There are so many souls there to be won for Jesus. "

Mary soon got over her sickness and was well and strong again. Now she went to the churches in Scotland to tell about the missionary work in Calabar. She made many friends. Some of the young people who heard her wanted to become missionaries. Miss Hoag, Miss Wright and Miss Peabody decided to become missionaries and later worked in Calabar, too.

Mary was so successful in interesting the people in mission work that the Board of Missions asked her to stay longer and visit more churches. Mary did what the Board asked, although she was anxious to get back to Africa. At last this work was finished. Now she could go back.

Mary was getting ready to go back to Africa when her sister Janie became sick.

"You will have to take her to a warmer climate, " said the doctor. "That is the only way she will get well. "

Mary could not afford to take her sister to Italy or southern France.

"I will ask the Board of Missions if I can take my sister with me to Africa. "

Anxiously Mary waited for an answer to her letter. At last the letter came.

We are sorry, but we must answer your question with a No. We feel that to take your sick sister along to Africa would be an unwise mixing of family problems and missionary work.

What should Mary do now? A friend told her to take her sister to southern England where the climate was warmer than in Scotland. She wrote to the Board to ask whether they would let her be a missionary if she took out the time to take care of her sister. The Board of Missions wrote:

Dear Miss Slessor:

When the way is clear for you to return to Calabar we will be glad to send you out again as our missionary. In the meantime we will be glad to pay your missionary salary for three more months.

Mary was glad that she could go back again, but she would not take the missionary salary when she was not working as a missionary. This left her with a sick sister and no salary. She took her sister Janie and her mother to southern England. They had been there only a short time when Mary's sister, Susan, in Scotland, died. It made her sad to lose a sister, but she was happy in the thought that Susan was now with Jesus her Saviour in Heaven.

After a while Janie was better and Mary packed up and got ready to sail once more to Africa. Just as she got ready to go, her mother became sick. What should Mary do now? She took her troubles to God in prayer. As she prayed, a thought came to her which showed her a way out of her problem.

"I will send for my old friend in Dundee to come and take care of Mother and then I can go to Africa. "

Mother Slessor agreed that this was the thing to do. Soon the friend came and now Mary was free to go to Africa. The weeks at sea were a good rest for her and she was in the best of health when she landed once more at Duke Town. Ten years had gone by since she first came to Africa.

"Where should I go now? " asked Mary of Daddy Anderson after she was once again in the mission house on Mission Hill.

"This time you are being sent up to Creek Town, " said Daddy Anderson.

"Oh, I'm glad, " said Mary. "That is the settlement farthest up the river. "

"You will work with the Rev. and Mrs. H. Goldie, " continued Daddy Anderson.

"That makes me happy, too. They are old friends. I met them on the trip the time before this one. "

As soon as she was settled in Creek Town, Mary worked harder than ever for the salvation of the natives. She did not care about her health. The only thing she could think of was how she could win more of the natives to Christ. She spent very little on herself because the money from her salary was needed back home in Scotland.

One day very sad news came from Scotland. Mother Slessor had died. Mary was very sad. Her mother was the one who had interested her in missionary work by telling her stories about it when she was only a little girl. Her mother had always encouraged her in her work. Her mother was willing to do anything and suffer anything so that Mary could be in the work of saving souls. Her mother was always interested in everything that Mary did. No wonder Mary was sad even though she knew that her mother was now with the Saviour in Heaven.

"There is no one to write and tell my stories and troubles and nonsense to. All my life I have been caring and planning and living for my mother and sisters. I am now left stranded and alone. "

But she was not alone. The words of Jesus, "Lo, I am with you alway, " came as sweet comfort to her heart.

"Heaven is now nearer to me than Scotland, " she said. "And no one will be worried about me if I go up country into the jungles. "

Mary was very anxious to go to the deep jungles to Okoyong, but every time she mentioned it the Board and the Andersons said, "No, not yet. " The tribes were cruel and wicked. They were always fighting among themselves and with other tribes. They did more bad and nasty things than any of the tribes she had ever worked with. They killed twin babies. They stole slaves and when they caught some stranger they made him a slave. They would hide along jungle paths and when someone went by, they would kill him. They hated the people of Calabar and the British government.

At different times missionaries had tried to get into this land, but always they had to run for their lives. The natives of Okoyong trusted no one. It was to that country that Mary wanted to carry the love of Jesus and the story that He died for them. Every day she would pray:

"Lord, if this is Your time, let me go. "

Meanwhile Mary worked hard at Creek Town. Besides her missionary work she was taking care of a number of native children. Some were twins she had saved from death, some were the children of slaves. Mary took care of these children at her own expense. In order to take care of them and have enough food for them, she ate only the simplest of foods, sometimes nothing but rice for a long time.

One day a man came to Creek Town to see Mary.

"I am the father of Janie, the twin, " he said. "I am glad you have taken care of her. "

"Come and see her, " said Mary.

"No, no! " said the man, "the evil spirit will put a spell on me. "

"You won't be hurt if you stand far away and look at her, " said Mary.

As he watched Janie, Mary took him by the arm and dragged him to the little girl. She put his strong black arms around her little shoulders. At last the man took the little girl on his lap and played and talked with her. After this he came often to visit his little girl and brought her food and presents. At last the time came when word reached Calabar that the Mission Board had decided that the Gospel should be preached in Okoyong and that Mary could go. Mary was very happy. At last God had answered her prayer. She was going into a wild country. She was going to go ahead of the other missionaries to find a place where they could build a mission house and church.

When King Eyo Honesty VII heard of it, he came to see Mary.

"So you are going into the wild country, to Okoyong, " he said.

"Yes, and I am so happy. Those people need to have their hearts and lives changed. I am happy that I shall be able to tell them about the Saviour. "

"Aren't you afraid to go among these wicked men? What if they should go on the warpath when you arrive? "

"I am not worried. God is on my side. If it is His will, He can keep me from all harm. If it is His will that I should die, then His will be done. If giving my life will help open Okoyong to the Gospel, I will gladly give it. "

"God bless you, Ma. I am going to let you use the king's canoe for this trip. My rowers can take you there swiftly. They will do anything you ask, because they love you. "

"Thank you, King Eyo; that will help me very much. "

King Eyo fixed up his canoe for Mary, as though she were a queen. He put a carpet in it, and many cushions. He put a sort of tent on it so that Mary could be alone when she wanted to be. The boat was loaded with homemade bread, canned meat, rice, and tea.

At last everything was ready for the trip into the wild country. Mary said good-by to her friends, the missionaries, and to her native friends. Then the thirty-five rowers pushed out from the shore and headed upstream toward the wild country. On both sides of the river were banana and palm trees. There were beautiful plants and flowers of many colors. The light shimmered on the flowing river as the rowers pulled the oars and sang their songs.

"What will happen if the Okoyongs are on the warpath? " Mary asked herself. "What will I do then? " Mary knew the answer. "I will put my trust in God and not in man. "

She lay back on the cushions and prayed to God to protect her in the wild country and to lead her in His way. The rowers rowed swiftly and sent the canoe shooting up the river toward the wild country.

"There is the landing place, " said the chief rower. "Now we must walk the rest of the way to Ekenge. "

Mary got out of the boat. The rowers followed her. They carried the packages Mary had brought with her. They began to walk through the jungle. It was four miles to Ekenge where Chief Edem lived. As they came near to the little village of mud huts, the chief rower whispered to Mary,

"There is Chief Edem. Praise God, he is at home and sober. "

Mary, too, thanked God that the Okoyongs were not on the warpath and she asked God's blessing on her visit with them.

When the people of Ekenge saw Mary they began to jump up and down and shout,

"Welcome, Ma. Welcome to Ekenge. "

Chief Edem bowed to her and said, "You are welcome Ma Mary. It is an honor to have you come to us. We are happy because you did not come with soldiers. We know now that you trust us. I have set aside a house for you as long as you stay with us. "

"Thank you, Chief Edem. I am happy to be here. "

"This is my sister, Ma Eme, " said the chief. Mary liked Ma Eme at once and Ma Eme liked Mary. They were friends as long as they lived.

"I want to go to visit the next village now, " said Mary. "I want to go to Ifako. "

"Oh, no, Ma, " said Chief Edem. "The chief is a very bad man. He is not fit for you to meet. Besides he is drunk now and he doesn't know what is going on. You must stay at Ekenge. "

"Very well, " said Mary, "I will stay, but call the people together so that I can have a Jesus-talk. "

When the people had all come together, Mary told about God's great love for them. She told them about Jesus who died that they might be saved. She told them about the happiness Jesus would bring to their village by changing their lives when they came to Him.

That night Mary did not sleep very much. The chief had given her one of the best houses in the village, but we would not think it was much of a house. Her bed was made of a few sticks with some corn shucks thrown over them. In the room all night were plenty of rats and insects. But Mary's heart was happy.

Later Mary went to Ifako. The chief there liked Mary very much. He and Chief Edem agreed to let her start a mission in their villages. Each one promised to give her ground for a schoolhouse and a mission house. Mary chose the places for the buildings. They were a half-hour's walk apart.

"Now I must go back to Creek Town, " said Mary. "When I come back again, it will be to stay. "

"Come soon, Ma, " said Chief Edem. "It will make us very happy to have you stay with us. "

As they rode down the river, Mary could not sleep at first because the rowers kept whispering,

"Don't shake the canoe or you will wake Ma, " or "Don't talk so loud so Ma can sleep. " At last, however, tired from her days of work in Ekenge and Ifako, she fell asleep and did not wake up until she came back to Creek Town.

Now she was very busy getting ready to move to Ekenge. One of the traders heard about her going to Ekenge.

"Do you trust those wild people? " he asked. "Do you think you can change them? What they need more than a missionary is a gun-boat to tame them down. "

"No, my friend, " answered Mary, "they need the same thing that every person in the world needs and that is the Saviour Jesus Christ. Only Jesus can change the hearts of sinful people. "

At last Mary was packed up. She was taking with her the five children she had saved from death. Another missionary, Mr. Bishop, was going along with her. Now at last Mary was going to work in the jungles as she had wanted to do. She had been in Africa for twelve years. She was now forty years old.

When Mary was ready to leave, all the people of Creek Town gathered around her. They told her good-by and wished her God's blessing.

"We will pray for you, " they said.

One of the young men she had taught in school said, "I will pray for you, but remember you are asking for death when you go to that wild country. "

It was getting dark when Mary's boat landed near Ekenge. The rain was pouring down. It was a four-mile walk to Ekenge. Mary and the five children started out. Mr. Bishop and the men who carried the baggage were to follow.

An eleven-year-old boy was in the lead. He was the oldest of the five children. He carried on his head a box filled with tea, sugar, and bread. An eight-year-old child followed him carrying a teakettle and cooking pots. Next came a three-year-old who held tight to little Janie's hand. Then came Mary carrying a baby girl and a bundle of food.

The children slipped in the mud. They became soaked by the rain. The jungle was dark around them and strange noises came from all sides. The children began to cry. They were hungry and scared.

"Don't cry children, " said Mary. "Remember Jesus is watching over us. He will take care of us. Soon we will be in the village and then we can have something to eat and we can put on dry clothes. "

They marched on. At last they came to the village. The village was dark and still. "Hello, hello, " called Mary. "Is anyone here? "

No one answered. Mary called again. At last two slaves came.

"Ma, " said the oldest slave, "the chief did not know you were coming today. The mother of the chief at Ifako died and all the people have gone to Ifako for the burying. "

"All right, " said Mary. "We will wait here then for Mr. Bishop and the baggage carriers. "

"I will send a messenger to Chief Edem, " said the slave, "to tell him that you have come. "

Mary took some of her food and cooked it over an open fire in the pouring rain. She fed the children and put them to bed.

At last Mr. Bishop came to the village.

"I am sorry, Miss Slessor, " he said. "The carriers will not bring anything until tomorrow. They are tired. They are afraid of the jungle trail. "

"But tomorrow is Sunday, " said Mary. "It would be a bad example for them to do work for us on Sunday. I will not have them work tomorrow. "

"John, " said Mary, turning to a young man who had come with Mr. Bishop, "you go back and tell the carriers they must come tonight for we need food and dry clothing. "

After the young man had gone, Mary decided she should go and help. She took off her muddy shoes and started back through the dark and fearful jungle. Mary was afraid when she heard the snarls of animals in the jungle, but she put her trust in God and went on.

As Mary came near to the beach she met John.

"Ma Mary, " he said, "the men will not come. They will not bring the things until the daylight chases away the hidden dangers of the jungle. "

"I will talk to them, " said Mary. She plodded on through the mud. She came to the canoe. The men were all sound asleep. Mary woke them and put them to work. In the meantime Mr. Bishop had coaxed some of the slaves from Ekenge to help. Soon all the things Mary had brought were being carried to Ekenge.

Sunday morning was cloudy. Mary got things ready for church. Church time came. But where were the people? Mary and Mr. Bishop and the children began to sing hymns as loud as they could. Still no one came. How discouraging! All the people had been at the burying. When they buried somebody, especially somebody important like the chief's mother, they would have a wild party. The people would get drunk and do many other wicked things. The next day they would be too tired and sick to do anything.

Mary and the children and Mr. Bishop kept on singing. At last a few women came. Mary gathered them around her and told them the story of Jesus and His love. The women listened but they did not say anything.

After the service was over and the women had gone to their huts, Mary knelt down and prayed.

"O God, my heavenly Father, with Your help I have made a beginning in the jungles of Okoyong. Things look black and discouraging now, but I know that if it is Your will You can change all that. If it is not Your will that my work is successful here, then send me wherever I can work best for You. Forgive my sins. Make me a better and more faithful worker for You. And bless the work here in Okoyong. I ask this for Jesus' sake. Amen. "

Would the work in Okoyong be a failure or a success? Time would tell. Mary knew that it depended on God.

At last Chief Edem and his people came back from the wild, drunken party at Ifako.

"Welcome Ma Mary, " said Chief Edem. "I am glad you have come. I have a place for you. You take this room here in my women's yard. It is for you. "

"Thank you, Chief, " said Mary. It was a dirty, filthy room, but it was the kind of room all the people of Okoyong used. Mary cleaned out the dirt. She had a window put in. She hung a curtain over the door. While she was working a boy came up to her.

"Ma Mary, " he said, "I am Ipke. I want to help you. " Ipke worked hard. He helped Mary as much as possible. Whatever there was to do, Ipke was ready to do it.

A few days later Mary looked out of her room. She saw Ipke. He was standing near a pot of boiling oil. A crowd of people stood around yelling and shouting.

Chief Edem came up to the crowd. Then a man took a dipper and filled it full of boiling oil. Ipke stretched out his hands in front of him. Suddenly Mary knew what was happening. She rushed out of her house, but she was too late. Already the man had poured the boiling oil over Ipke's arms and hands.

"Why have you done this? " asked Mary. Chief Edem said nothing. He turned and walked away. The other people also kept still. Mary took Ipke to her room. She put medicine on the burns.

"Why did they do this to you, Ipke? " she asked.

"It is because I helped the white Ma. The people say I do not follow the old ways. It is bad to follow new ways. I must be punished. The bad spirit must be burned out. "

"O God, " prayed Mary, "heal this boy and help me to change the wicked heathen ways. "

6

A Brave Nurse

It was strangely quiet in the village of Chief Okurike. The chief was sick. All the magic of the witch doctors could not make him better. If he died, many of his wives, slaves and soldiers would be killed to go with him into the spirit-world.

A woman from a neighboring village came to the house of Chief Okurike's wives.

"You are sad because Chief Okurike is dying, " said the woman. "I know someone who can help him. Far away through the jungle at Ekenge lives the white Ma. With her magic she can make devils go out of your chief. My son's child was dying. The white Ma saved her. She is well today. The white Ma has done many wonderful things by the power of her juju. Let your chief send for her. Then he will not die. "

The wives talked it over.

"We must tell the chief, " said the head wife. "He must send for the white Ma. If he dies, many of us must die too. We do not want to die."

They told the chief about the strange white Ma at Ekenge.

"Let her be sent for, " said the chief. "Send swift runners to ask her to come. "

All day long the men hurried through the jungle along the narrow paths. They went through many villages but they did not stop. At last after eight hours, they came to the village of Ekenge.

"We are the men of Chief Okurike, " said the men to Chief Edem. "Chief Okurike is very sick. We want the white Ala who lives in your village to come and heal him. "

"She will say for herself what she will do, " said Chief Edem. He sent a man to tell Mary some men from Chief Okurike wanted to see her. Mary came at once to see what was wanted.

"Ma, " said the men, "Chief Okurike sent us. He is very sick. Come and bring your magic medicines and make him well. "

"What kind of sickness does your chief have? " asked Mary. "Maybe I can send the medicine with you. "

They shook their heads. They did not know what the sickness was.

"I must help, " said Mary to herself. "If the chief dies, then according to their heathen way the tribe will kill all his wives and slaves so he will have company on the long trip to the spirit-world. I must go and teach them about the Good Shepherd who is with us even in the valley of the shadow of death. If the chief should die and the tribe think that it is because of witchcraft it will be even worse. Many people will be killed because the tribe will think they used witchcraft to kill the chief. "

"I will go with you, " said Mary.

"There are warriors out in the jungle and you will be killed. You must not go, " said Chief Edem.

"It is a long journey, " said Ma Eme. "There are deep rivers to cross. It is raining very hard. You will never get there. "

"If Chief Okurike dies, there will be fighting and killing. You will be in great danger, " said Chief Edem. "Don't go. "

Mary knew that if anything happened to her, Chief Edem would go to war against the tribe of Chief Okurike, because she was his guest, and a chief must protect his guest. Mary prayed to God about it. Then she said to Chief Edem, "I am sure that God wants me to go. It will be a chance to tell these people about Jesus who heals the soul-sickness. God will take care of me. "

"Well, Ma, I do not like it, but you may go if you wish. I will send women with you to look after you. I will send men to protect you. "

Early the next morning they started on the journey. It was raining hard. After they had left Ekenge, it began to pour. The jungle was flooded and steaming hot. It was hard to go, but Mary and the guard pushed on. Soon Mary's clothes were soaked through. They became so heavy she could hardly walk. Her boots became water soaked. She took them off and threw them in the bush. Soon her stockings wore out and she walked through the jungle mud barefooted. She knew she was doing God's work, and even fearful rainstorms were not going to stop her.

After three hours the weather began to clear, but now Mary's head began to ache from fever. As Mary and the guard passed through the jungle villages, the people looked at Mary with surprise. But nothing would stop Mary. She pushed on, and after walking through the jungle for eight hours, she stumbled into the village of the sick chief.

Some of the people were crying. They expected to be killed when the chief died. Others were laughing and shouting. They were going to have "fun" when the chief died. They were going to kill people and have a wild party.

Mary was tired and sick, but she went at once to the chief's house. He was stretched out on a dirty bed. His face was gray with sickness. He was moaning and groaning. He was very near death.

Mary examined the chief to see what his sickness was. She opened her little medicine chest and took out some medicine. She gave the chief a dose. It made the chief a little better.

"I don't have enough of this medicine with me, " said Mary. She knew that away on the other side of the river another missionary was working. She knew he had some of the medicine. She went to the men of the village.

"You must go across the river to Ikorofiong for more medicine, " said Mary.

"No, no, we cannot go, " said the men of the village. "Our enemies are on the other side of the river. They will kill us if we go there. "

"But I must have the medicine, " said Mary.

"There is a man from that village down the river a little ways. He is living in his canoe on the river. Maybe he will go, " said one of the men.

Some of the men ran down to the river. They found the man. They promised him many things. At last he said he would go. The next day he brought the medicine to Mary.

For days Mary nursed Chief Okurike. She taught one of his wives how to help her. She also told the chief and his family about Jesus. Whenever she could leave the chief for a short time she would talk to the tribe about the Saviour and how He would change their lives if they believed in Him.

Day after day Mary prayed for Chief Okurike. At last prayer won out. Chief Okurike got well. The people were very happy.

"Ma Mary, " they said, "we want to learn book. " They meant that they wanted to learn about the Bible.

"I am glad you do, " said Mary, "but then you must do what the Book says. "

"We will, " said the people. "We will make peace with Calabar. We will not kill the traders who come to our land or the other white people. "

"Then I will always be your worker and I will send you a teacher as soon as I can, who will teach you of the Saviour who died for you to pay for your sins. "

Mary went back to Ekenge. Here she found that Chief Edem was very sick. He had some very bad boils on his back. Mary put medicine on the boils. Every day she came to his house and took care of him. One day when she came in she saw feathers and eggs lying around the room. This was witch doctor "medicine. " On the Chief's neck and around his arms and legs were witch charms.

"Oh, Chief Edem, " said Mary, "how could you do this? Surely you know that doing witchcraft is a sin against God. I do not see how you could go back to it after you had learned to know about Jesus. "

"Ma, you don't know all about these things. Someone is the cause of this sickness. You don't know all the badness of the black man's heart. Look, here are the proofs that someone is working witchcraft against me. The only one who can fight that is the witch doctor. He is the only one who can make me well. See, here are the things that were taken from my back. "

Chief Edem pointed to a collection of shot, egg shells, seed and other things which the witch doctor said had come from his back. He believed the witch doctor. He believed that someone using witchcraft had sent them into his back.

Mary knew what would happen. Everybody whom the chief thought might have done the witchcraft would have to take poison. The people thought that if the person who took the poison died, he was guilty, but if he was not guilty he would live. The tribe would also use other tortures like pouring boiling oil on people to get them to confess.

"That is all wrong, " said Mary. "The sickness is because you have not eaten good things or taken care of yourself and kept as clean as you should have. Don't believe the bad witch doctor. " (God said something about that in Exodus 22:18.)

Chief Edem would not listen. He had everyone he thought might have the witchcraft made a prisoner. The witch doctor took the chief and his wives and chief men and prisoners to a nearby farm. Mary was not allowed to come to this farm.

Mary knew of Someone who could help her. She prayed to God again and again to keep these people from doing the bad things they planned. Days went by. Mary prayed that Chief Edem might get well. God heard Mary's prayers. He did what she asked. He made Chief Edem well again.

When Chief Edem was well again he decided not to kill the prisoners, the people he thought might have done witchcraft against him. He let them go free. Then the chief and his wives and the chief men came back to the village.

The tribe had a big party to celebrate. They were happy the chief was well. It was the wildest party Mary had ever seen. The people stuffed themselves with food until they became sick. They got drunk. They had wild dances. They did many wicked things.

Mary had often prayed that God would turn the heathen people from their wicked ways, but here they were carrying on worse than ever. The only answer to her prayers that she could see was that the prisoners who were going to be killed had been set free.

"Am I doing anything for my Saviour? " Mary asked herself. "Am I having any success in winning people for Jesus? "

7

Witchcraft

One day Chief Njiri and his warriors came to visit Chief Edem. They stayed several days. They had wild parties every day. They drank native beer until they became drunk. Then they would quarrel and fight. They asked Mary to settle their quarrels and decide who was right. Mary was praying every day that there would not be bad fights and that no one would be killed.

Finally it was the last night of the visit. The men were so drunk that Mary knew there would be trouble. When the chief and his men were ready to leave, everyone was excited. The people were shouting and pushing. Some shots were fired and the men began stabbing with their swords. They were too drunk to know what they were doing. Mary ran into the crowd. She went up to Chief Njiri.

"Chief, " said Mary, "your visit is over. Go now before trouble starts. " She took hold of the chief's arm and led him out of the village and his men followed him. They started for their own village.

"I'm glad that's over, " said Mary, but she had spoken too soon.

On their way home, as they were staggering along, Bakulu, one of Njiri's men, cried out, "Look! " and pointed with his finger. The chief and his men stopped.

"It is witchcraft, " said Bakulu. "See the little banana plant with palm leaves, nuts and a coconut shell close by! "

"Don't go past it, " said one of the other men. "It is bad medicine. You will get sick and die. "

"It is the people in the last village we passed through. They did it. Let us punish them, " said Chief Njiri.

"Yes, let's punish them, " shouted the men. Mary had been following the men to make sure they would go home.

She heard the shouting. Now the men started running past her. She tried to stop them, but they slipped away. Mary took a short cut through the jungle. She reached the road to the village before the men did.

"God, our Father in Heaven, " prayed Mary, "help me for Jesus' sake to stop these men, so there will not be a bloody battle. "

"Stop, " she cried as the first men came in sight. "Stop, I want to talk to you. "

The men stopped. The others soon came running up. They had to stop, too.

"You men are planning to do something bad. You do not know that the people of this village did bad things to you. You only think they did. You have drunk too much beer. You do not know what you are doing. Go home. "

"But Ma, " said Njiri, "they have made bad medicine against us. They made witchcraft. They must be punished before we are hurt. "

Njiri and his men argued with Mary, but finally they listened to her. They turned around and once more started for home. Mary went with them to make sure they would get there. At last they came again to the banana plant and the witch medicine. They were afraid to pass it.

"If we pass it, we will get sick and die, " said Njiri.

"That is sinful foolishness, " said Mary. "That banana plant and those other things will not hurt you. I am not afraid of them. "

Mary picked up the banana plant, the palm leaves, nuts and coconut shell and threw them into the jungle.

"Now, brave men, come on. I have cleared the path. Let us go to your village. "

Timidly the men tiptoed past the place where the "medicine" had been. Then they went on to their own village. Once more Mary thought that all would be peaceful now for a while. She started for the village of Ekenge.

No sooner was Mary gone than the people of Njiri began drinking again. Then they started quarreling and fighting. One of the men in the village ran and told Mary.

"I will fix that, " said Mary. She took some of the men of Ekenge with her. She went to the village of Njiri. With the help of the men of Ekenge and some of the people of the village, they tied some of the most drunken men and the wildest fighters to the trees. They left them there to cool themselves in the breezes of the jungle.

After several hours Mary untied them because she was afraid that some lions might come and kill and eat them. Now that things were quiet, Mary again started for home. On the way she picked up the little banana plant that had caused so much trouble and took it with her.

"I will plant it in my own yard and see what witchcraft can do! " said Mary.

Early the next morning, a man from Njiri's village came running into Ekenge. He went to Mary's house.

"Ma, " said the runner, "Chief Njiri was very sick last night. He suffered very much. The witch doctor took sticks and shells and shot from his leg. It is because he walked past the banana plant and other magic medicine. Give me the little banana plant for the chief. "

"No, I cannot do that, " said Mary. She knew that if the banana plant was taken to the chief, someone would die because of the witchcraft belief.

"But you must send it, " said Chief Edem. "If you do not send it, he will make war on us. "

"Very well, " said Mary, "I will send it. But I know there will be much trouble. "

So he took the banana plant to Chief Njiri. When he received it, he and his warriors went to the village which he thought was working witchcraft against him. He made all the people of the village come to him. In great fear they came.

"Every one of you must swear that you did not make that bad medicine against me. I am going to find out who is working that witchcraft to hurt me. "

All the people of the village swore they had not done it.

"I am going to take one of your finest young men with me. If I find that you have told me a lie, I will kill him. "

Njiri's warriors captured a young man and took him along. If the villagers had tried to rescue him, he would have been killed, and many of them would have been killed also. They sent a man to Mary.

"Ma, " said the man, "please help us. Please get Njiri to free Kolu. "

"I don't like to have anything to do with Njiri. He is very wicked. But I will go and try to get Kolu free. "

Mary went to the village of Chief Njiri. She walked right up to the chief. The warriors of Chief Njiri looked at her with angry faces. They shook their spears at her.

"Chief Njiri, " said Mary, "why have you taken this young man? He has done you no harm. You are doing a bad thing. "

"Ha, ha, " laughed Chief Njiri. "Do you think I am so foolish, Ma? I know these people put bad medicine in my path. I saw the sticks and shells which the witch doctor took from my leg. If sickness comes, I will kill this man. "

"The village people have sworn to you that they did not put those things in your path, " said Mary.

"Perhaps they are lying. "

"They are not lying, but you have lied. You promised to go home and not harm these people. You lied to me. You have made trouble. You went to their village and made them swear. You stole this young man. It is wrong to lie. God will surely punish those who speak with a lying tongue. Please set this young man free so that he may return to his village and his people. "

"Ma, " answered Chief Njiri, "you do not understand these things. You do not know the badness in the hearts of these people. You do not know the bad things they want to do against me. You do not know about witchcraft. "

"Oh, yes, I do, " said Mary. "I know that God will punish those who do witchcraft. He will punish those who are foolish enough to believe in it. The people who trust in Jesus do not fear witchcraft. Why do you not trust in Jesus? "

"I don't need Jesus. I am a strong chief. I have many warriors. No one can harm me. "

"If no one can hurt you, why don't you set this young man free? "

"I will not set him free. If I keep him, his people will be afraid even to try hurting me. "

"But think, Chief, how you would feel if you were captured and taken away from your people? Think how sad this young man feels. Great chiefs show mercy and kindness to the weak. Will you show mercy and kindness to the people of the village and free this young man? "

"A great chief is not weak. He does not act like a woman. A woman shows kindness and love. I am not weak. I will punish. I will revenge myself on those who would do evil to me. "

"Revenge belongs to the true and powerful God. He will punish those who do evil. I beg you, Chief Njiri, to set this man free. "

"Ma, if I were not a good chief I would have killed you a long time ago. But go now. I do not want to hear your talk. I will not set this young man free. Maybe I will kill him. Maybe I will not kill him. But I will not set him free. Go, before I become angry with you. "

"I will go, but remember Chief Njiri, the great and powerful God who sees and knows the badness in your heart. He knows the evil you do. Please turn to Him and believe in Him before it is too late and you end in Hell, the place where bad people suffer forever. "

"Go, " said Chief Njiri angrily, "get out of my village. Go back to Ekenge. "

Sadly Mary started back to Ekenge.

"I have failed these people who asked for my help. O God, soften the heart of Chief Njiri and keep Your protecting hand over the young man Kolu. "

When Chief Edem heard that Njiri would not set the man free, he said,

"Njiri has insulted our Ma. Let the warriors get their spears and shields. Let us get ready for war. "

The women slipped quietly into Mary's room to tell her the latest news. It made Mary sad that these men were getting ready for a war, but neither one of the chiefs would listen to her. Mary knew where to go for help. She prayed to God.

"O God, " prayed Mary, "You can stop this war. You can soften the hearts of these cruel chiefs. Please stop this war so that the warriors may not be killed and their wives made widows and their children orphans. Hear me for the sake of Jesus, my Saviour. "

A man knocked on the door of Mary's hut. "Ma, Ma, " he cried, "Kolu has been set free. Chief Njiri let him go, and he is back at the village. There will be no war! "

"Thank You, Father in Heaven, " prayed Mary. "Thank You that You heard my prayers and that peace and quiet will again be in the villages. "

Mary had a true friend in Ma Eme, the sister of Chief Edem. She helped Mary often. She did everything she could to help Mary and the mission, but one thing she never did, that was to confess Christ openly. She and Mary talked of many things as they worked together. One day Ma Eme said,

"When my husband died, I had to go through the chicken test. "

"What is that? " asked Mary.

"All of my husband's wives, I too, were put on trial. The witch doctors were trying to find who caused my husband, a great chief, to die. Each of us had to bring a chicken. The witch doctor chopped off the heads of the chickens one at a time. If the headless chicken fluttered one way, the witch doctor said the wife was innocent. If it fluttered the other way, he said she was guilty. "

"What happened when they cut off the head of your chicken? " asked Mary.

"It fluttered wildly in the right direction. The witch doctor said I was innocent. But the strain had been so great I fainted and had to be carried to my hut. But many of the other wives were killed. "

"You do not believe in the witch doctors, do you? " asked Mary.

Ma Eme looked all around. Then she stepped close to Mary and whispered, "No, but I would not tell anyone else. They are too strong and tricky. They could cause me much trouble if they knew I was against them. "

"I shall fight the witch doctors as long as God gives me strength. God is against the witch doctors who do such evil things. "

Chief Edem had promised Mary a house, and the people of the village had said they would build it. But whenever Mary wanted to start, they would say, "Tomorrow, we will start, Ma. " But tomorrow just did not come.

At last Mary and the children she had adopted and the native children cleared the ground. They stuck sticks in the ground for the wall. They began to make the roof. Then some of the lazy people of the village began to help, and at last the house was built.

Mary also wanted to build a church and school at Ifako. The chief there had promised to help. But the people of that village were lazy, too. They were always putting off doing the building. One morning a man came from Ifako.

"My master wants you, " he said.

Mary went to Ifako. The chiefs were together at a cleared piece of ground.

"See, Ma, here is your ground. Here are the sticks, and mud, and palm leaves and other things we need to build. Shall we build the church today? "

It did not take long for Mary to say yes. The people of the village forgot to be lazy. They were having fun building the church. When it was finally finished it was twenty-five feet wide by thirty feet long. We would not think that was a very big building, but it was the biggest in the village.

"See, " said the Chief of Ifako, "it is much better than the house at Ekenge. "

"It is a fine church, " said Mary. "Now we must keep it clean and nice. There should be no dirty things in or around God's house. "

We would not think it was such a fine church. The walls were made of dry mud and sticks. The roof was made of palm-leaf mats. The floors were made of mud and so were the seats. But everything was polished and rubbed as smooth as possible. There were no windows or doors in the building. There were just holes in the wall to let in the light for windows and a larger hole to serve as an entrance. But Mary thought it was a fine church because it was the best in that part of the country and because it was a place where people could hear about the Saviour and learn "book. "

"We will hold our first service in the new church next Sunday, " said Mary. "I want you all to come. "

"We will come, Ma, " promised the natives.

8

The Poison Test

"Tomorrow we will have our first service in our new church. You must dress right for it, " said Mary.

She took out of her mission boxes clothes of all kinds and colors which the people in the homeland had sent to her.

"You must wear these to church tomorrow, " said Mary. "In God's house you must be clean. You must be dressed. You must not bring your spears into church. "

"Can we come? " asked the children.

"Indeed you can, " said Mary. "The children can come and the slaves can come. God's house is open to everyone. "

The next day was indeed a happy day for Mary. The church was filled with people. Many of them came just out of curiosity, but there were many who had learned to know and love and trust in Jesus.

Mary now started day classes and these too were crowded because many wanted to learn "book. " They wanted to learn about Ma's God and about the Saviour who took away sins. It was not long before a change could be seen in many of these people. They had become Christians. The look of fear was gone from their eyes. They no longer feared the demons because they had a Saviour who loved them and took care of them. They did not do the wicked things they had done before. They tried to live as God wanted them to live.

Mary was happy. Now she wanted to build a larger and better mission house in Ekenge. Chief Edem wanted that too. He felt that the church schoolhouse in Ifako quite outshone the little two-room house in Ekenge. Mary wanted doors and windows in the new house. She could not make them. The natives could not. They had never seen any.

Mary wrote to the Mission Board about it. The Mission Board put a notice in the magazine they published asking for a practical carpenter who was willing to go to Calabar. Mr. Charles Ovens saw the notice.

"This is God's call to me, " he said. "I have wanted to be a missionary ever since I was a little boy. I could not study to be a minister. I learned to be a carpenter. Now I can be a carpenter for God. I can build mission houses and churches and while I build I can tell the people about my Saviour. "

It was in May, 1889, that Mr. Ovens started for Calabar. In Duke Town he found a native helper and the two of them went to Ekenge. Mary was very glad to have him come. He was a very jolly man. He sang at his work. Everyone liked him and the natives gladly helped him in building the houses.

For a long time Mary had been trying to get the chiefs of Okoyong to trade with the traders on the coast. They would not listen. Now she invited them to her new house. She showed them the things she had and how useful they were. The chiefs looked at the door and windows. They liked them. The women looked at the clothes and at the sewing machine. They liked them. They looked at the clock on the mantel. They liked it, too.

"We will trade with coast people, " said Chief Edem.

Mary wrote to the traders and invited them to Okoyong. She told them to bring dishes, dress goods, mirrors, clocks, and the like to trade for ivory, oil, and bananas and other things in the jungle.

"It is too dangerous to come up-country, " answered the traders. "We are afraid the native guards on the jungle paths will kill us. "

Mary wrote to good King Eyo, of Duke Town. She asked him to invite the Okoyong chiefs for a conference. She promised they would bring jungle goods to trade.

King Eyo invited the chiefs. They did not want to go. Mary told them of the interesting things they would see on the coast. She told them of the good things they could get by trading. At last they agreed to go. They collected two canoeloads of bananas, barrels of oil and other jungle crops. Then the chiefs and warriors came marching down to the river to go to the coast.

"Wait, " said Mary. "You cannot take those spears and swords and guns along. You will only get into trouble. You must leave your swords and spears, your guns and knives at home. "

When Mary said this, many of the natives disappeared into the jungle. They would not go without their weapons.

"Ma, you make women of us, " argued those who remained. "Would a man go among strangers without arms? "

"You may not take arms, " said Mary. "You are not going to war. You are going for a friendly visit. "

"If we cannot take our swords and guns we will not go. We will stay home. "

"But you promised and I promised King Eyo that you would come. Will you go back on your word and make me a liar? "

For two hours they argued with Mary. The beach filled with natives from the village who wanted to see the chiefs start on their trip. The chiefs did not want to look like cowards to the people of the village. At last they took off their swords and gave their guns to their white Ma. Those who had run away to the jungle came back and decided to go along.

"We do not like this, " said the chiefs, "but we will go. We will not make you a liar, Ma. "

They got off into their boats. As one of the boats rowed off, one of the bags shifted. Mary saw the gleam of flashing swords.

"Stop! " cried Mary. The rowers stopped. Mary took the swords and threw them into the river.

"Shame on you, " said Mary. "I did not think you would try to fool me like that. " The chiefs said nothing. They just rowed down the river.

The chiefs who went to Duke Town had a wonderful time. They went to the church services. King Eyo Honesty talked with them about the Gospel and what it meant for their lives. He took them to his house and had a big dinner for them. They traded the bananas, oil, and other things which they had brought for things to take home like mirrors, clocks, and white people's clothes. Then the next day they rowed back to Ekenge.

The village people were all gathered down at the landing place to welcome the chiefs home. They watched patiently for the boats. When the boats came the people shouted for joy.

"Welcome home, Chief Edem, " said Mary. "How was your trip? Did you enjoy your visit at Duke Town? "

"The trip was fine, Ma, " said Chief Edem. "Duke Town is a big village. They have a big churchhouse. We saw many things. "

"Did you need your guns and swords? " asked Mary.

"No, Ma, you were right. We did not need guns or swords. King Eyo was good to us. We have many fine things. "

"If you work hard and get things to trade, you can get many more fine things, " said Mary.

"We are going to work hard. We want many of those fine things we saw. "

The men did work. Because they were busy they had less time and less desire to get drunk and quarrel. Mary's missionary work was having its effect on the lives of the people. Slowly they were changing from their heathen ways, but there was still much to do.

One day while Mary and Mr. Ovens were working on the mission house they heard a wild scream from the nearby jungle. Mary jumped up.

"Something is wrong in the jungle, " said Mary. "Johnny, go and see what it is. "

One of her orphan boys ran off to find out what was wrong. In a few minutes he came back.

"Ma, Ma, " he cried, "a man is hurt. Maybe he is dead. Come quick. "

Mary grabbed her case of medicines and followed Johnny into the jungle. When she reached the place where the young man was lying, she looked into his face.

"It is Etim, the son of our chief, Edem. He is going to get married soon and is building his house. A tree fell the wrong way and hit him. He cannot move his arms or legs. This means bad trouble. The people will say it is witchcraft. "

Mary with her helpers quickly made a stretcher to carry Etim. They carried him to his mother's home at Ekenge.

"I will nurse him, " said Mary to Etim's mother.

For two weeks Mary took care of him night and day. She prayed God to spare the young man's life. She did everything she knew to help him. Etim did not get better. Day by day he became worse. Sunday morning came. Mary could see that he did not have long to live. She left him for a short time to arrange for Mr. Ovens to take care of the church services. Hearing Etim groaning and crying out, she rushed back to the house where he was.

The natives were blowing smoke into his nose. They were rubbing pepper into his eyes. His uncle, Ekponyong, shouted into his ears. They thought they were helping him to get well. Instead they made him die sooner. In a moment he gave a cry and fell back dead.

"Etim is dead! " cried the people in the house. "Witches have killed him! They must die! Bring the witch doctor at once! "

The people who were in the house quickly disappeared, and soon only Mary and Etim's relatives were left. When the witch doctor came, he did all kinds of queer things, which he said would tell him who had made the young man die. He pretended to be listening to the dead boy talk.

"It is the people of Payekong. They are to blame. They put a spell on him, " said the witch doctor.

Chief Edem called for the leader of his soldiers.

"Take my warriors and go to Payekong, " said Chief E'dem. "Capture the people and burn down the houses. Quickly now! "

The warriors were too late. Chief Akpo, the chief of Payekong, had heard the news. He and his people had run off into the jungle. Only a few people were left in the village. Those were captured by Edem's soldiers and brought to Ekenge.

Mary was sure that Chief Edem would make the people take the poison bean test. This is how the test was made: A small brown bean full of poison was crushed and put into water. The person who was tested had to drink the poison water. The natives thought that if the person drank the water and died, he was guilty; if he lived, he was innocent.

"That is no way to honor your son, Chief Edem, " said Mary. "You know it is wrong and sinful to kill people. "

"But they are bad people. They deserve to die. "

"You do not know that. That water is poison. Anyone who drinks it would die. "

"Oh, no, Ma, if the one who drinks it is innocent he will live. "

"I do not agree with you. Come, let us honor your son in a better way. "

Mary wrapped the young man's body in silk. She dressed him in the finest suit she could find. She wrapped a silk turban around his head and then placed a high red and black hat with bright colored feathers on his head. No chief had ever been dressed so fine for his burial. The body was carried out into the yard and seated in a large chair under an umbrella. A silver-headed stick and a whip was placed in his hand. This showed he was a chief's son. A mirror was also put in his hand so he could see how wonderful he was. On a table beside him were placed all his treasures. Those included skulls he had taken in war. Then the people were let into the yard to see Etim.

The people shouted. They were so happy they danced around. They called for whiskey to drink. Chief Edem gave them much whiskey to drink. They became wilder and wilder.

Mary and Mr. Ovens took turns watching the prisoners. They were afraid the people would kill them. As Mary was going to her house for a little rest, she saw some poison beans on the pounding stone. This filled her with fear. She was not afraid for herself, but for the poor prisoners. She fell on her knees and prayed.

"Dear Father in Heaven, " prayed Mary, "watch over these poor people. Do not let harm come to these prisoners. Keep the other people from doing murder. Give me the courage to face the chiefs and tell them they are wrong. In all these things may Thy will be done. I ask this in Jesus' name. "

After she had prayed Mary got up and went to Chief Edem and his brother Ekponyong.

"You must forbid the poison bean test, " said Mary. "It is wrong and sinful. God is watching what you do. Do not do that sinful thing. "

"That is my business, " said Chief Edem. "I am the chief of this tribe. I will do what seems good to me. "

Mary argued with the chief, but he would not listen. Ekponyong, his brother, encouraged Edem to make the prisoners take the poison bean test. Mary then went to the yard where the prisoners were kept. She sat down in the gateway. She was not going to let anyone get the prisoners. This made the chiefs very angry. The crowd of village people howled and yelled. Chief Edem's warriors shook their swords and guns at her and stamped the ground angrily.

"Raise our master from the dead, " shouted the people, "and we will free the prisoners! "

Mary kept her place. She wrote a note to Duke Town asking for help and sent it off secretly by one of her orphan boys. Still she watched over the prisoners. She would not leave her place in the gate. The people were angry with her, but still many of them loved and respected their white Ma and would not hurt her. Suddenly a man pushed his way through the crowd. He shoved Mary aside. He grabbed one of the women prisoners. He dragged her in front of the body of Etim. He handed her the cup of poison.

"Drink! " he cried. "Drink and prove that you are innocent, or drink and die! "

9

Victories for Mary

"Oh ma, do not leave us. Please do not leave us, " begged the other prisoners as the poor woman prisoner got ready to drink the poison.

"Lord, help me and help these poor people, " prayed Mary.

Mary went up to the woman. The woman raised the cup of poison to her lips. Mary grabbed her arm.

"Run, " she whispered. "Run to the mission house. "

Before the crowd knew what was happening, Mary and the woman had run far into the jungle. They went to the mission house. No one would dare to harm anyone in the mission house. Mary then went back to the other prisoners.

"O God, I thank Thee that I was able to help this poor woman get away. Help me to save these other prisoners also. "

When Mary got back to the other prisoners, the argument with the chiefs started again.

"An innocent person will not die if he drinks the poison, " said Ekponyong. "Only a bad, guilty person will die. "

"That is not right, " answered Mary. "Poison will kill anyone, good or bad. Chief Edem, you know it was an accident that your son died. It was not the fault of any of these people. Please let them go free. "

"I want my son to be buried in a box like the white people, " said Chief Edem. "Will Bwana Ovens make a fine box for my son? "

"I will make a coffin for your son if you will let the prisoners go free, " said Mr. Ovens.

"No, no, " said Chief Edem.

"Then I will not make a box for you. "

"Well, then I will let some go free, " said Chief Edem.

"No, you must not let them go free, " said Ekponyong.

"If I want to let them go free, I can, " said Chief Edem. "I am chief, don't forget that. "

"Show that you are a great and wise chief, " said Mary. "Let them all go free. "

Chief Edem thought a while. Then he spoke.

"If Bwana Ovens will make a fine box for my son then I will let all go free but Mojo, Otinga, and Obwe, " said Chief Edem.

"But why keep them? " asked Mary.

"Mojo and Otinga are related to Etim's mother. They planned bad things against my boy. Obwe is related to Chief Akpo who has run away because he is guilty. Now if I let these others go will you build me a box Bwana Ovens? "

"Yes, I will build you a box, " said Mr. Ovens.

"Please let the three go free, too, " said Mary. "They have done you no wrong. "

"We have done more for you than we have ever done before. We will do nothing else, " said Chief Edem. He turned his back on Mary and walked away.

People from other villages came to take part in the wild parties that were always held when there was a funeral. Mary tried again and again to get Edem to free the three prisoners. Mary and Mr. Ovens managed to take Mojo and Otinga to the mission house where they were safe. Again Mary pleaded for Obwe. Chief Edem was very angry.

"Will you not have me honor my son? You have run off with my prisoners. I will burn down the mission house. I will send you back to Duke Town. Then you cannot trouble me any longer. "

"Brother, you do not speak wisely, " said Ma Eme, E'dem's sister. "The white Ma has done many good things for us. If we burn down the mission house you will have a bad name among all tribes. Chain Obwe in the white Ma's yard so that the village people cannot harm her. She cannot get away and you can find out later whether she is guilty or not. "

"Very well, " said Chief Edem, "I will do that. But the three must be killed for the funeral. What kind of a funeral will that be for a chief's son if no one is killed? He will have no one to go with him on the way to the dark land. "

The next day two missionaries came from Duke Town in answer to Mary's note. It was a great honor to have so many white people at a funeral. Chief Edem was no longer as angry as he had been. The missionaries showed slide pictures. The natives had never seen anything like it before. It pleased them very much and it also quieted them down. The next day when the funeral was held, a cow was killed and put in the coffin with Etim instead of the people who were thought to have worked witchcraft against him.

Mary was glad and thankful to God that she had been able to save the prisoners. The last of the prisoners was let go free on the promise that if Chief Akpo was caught he would take the poison test. Mary heard that Etim was the only chief in Okoyong ever to be buried without some people being killed as a human sacrifice. The people of the jungle thought Mary was wonderful indeed.

Mary thought that this trouble was over, but a short time later Etim's uncle, who lived in a nearby village, was accused of having killed the young man. He came to Ekenge and met with the village chiefs.

"I am willing to take the poison bean test, " said the uncle, "if all of the chiefs will take the test. That means you, too, Edem. Those who are innocent will not be hurt. I will take the test, but all the other chiefs must, too. "

When Mary heard that Etim's uncle was going to take the poison bean test if the other chiefs would, she rushed to the village. The men were arguing. They were shaking their swords and guns at one another. Mary looked around until she found the bag of poison beans. She took them and ran off with them.

The chiefs could not find the poison beans. Finally, they quieted down. Chief Edem went to Mary.

"Give me the poison beans, " he said. "I know you have taken them."

"Yes, I took them, " said Mary, "but I will not give them to you. There has been enough trouble and sadness and fear. When will you be satisfied that your son's death was an accident? "

Chief Edem turned around and went back to the village. He sent all the chiefs home. Nothing more was said about the poison bean test.

Now Mary began to plead for Akpo, the chief of the village which the witch doctor had said had caused Etim to be killed.

"Chief Edem, let him come home. Forgive him. He has done you no wrong. "

God softened Edem's heathen heart. After several weeks he agreed to let Akpo come home.

"You may tell him, " Edem said to Mary, "that all thought of revenge is gone from my heart. If he wishes to return to his own village, he may do so, or he may go anywhere in Okoyong in safety. "

Nothing like that had ever been done before in the jungle. The heathen people did not forgive. They always took revenge. Akpo did not believe Edem had forgiven him. He did not want to trust Edem. At last Mary convinced him that Edem meant just what he said and that Akpo could really go home.

Mary and Akpo came to his home village of Payekong. The houses had been burned. The cattle had been stolen. But it was still home. Tears came to Akpo's eyes. Thankfully the chief kneeled at Mary's feet.

"Oh, Ma, thank you, thank you for what you have done for me and my people. I and my people will always do whatever you ask. " Akpo kept his promise. Other chiefs often argued with Mary and threatened to hurt her, but Akpo and his people always helped her and did whatever she wanted them to do.

Chief Edem now was kind to Akpo and his people. He built houses for them and helped them get their gardens started again. He gave them some cattle, too. After some time had gone by, Chief Edem came to Mary. He kneeled down before her.

"Thank you, Ma, for being brave. Thank you for keeping after me until I let those prisoners go. I am glad that people were not killed at the time of Etim's death. Your ways are better than ours. We are tired of the old ways. "

Many other people came and told her how glad they were that the old ways were changing. They said that they knew the old ways were bad. Mary had had a very hard time in the jungles, but now things were going better. She was busy all the time, teaching and preaching and nursing. She journeyed through the jungle where the wild animals were, but she did not fear. She was trusting God to take care of her as He had taken care of Daniel in the lions' den. Always she told the people of the loving Saviour who had died for their sins.

After a time Mary fell sick. She caught the jungle fever. She became very weak.

"Mary, " said Ovens, "you must take a vacation. You must get away from the jungle for a while. You must go to England for a long rest. That way you can get well and come back to work here at Okoyong. "

"You are right, " said Mary. "Much as I hate to leave my work here, I know I must go. I will ask for a furlough at once. "

For three years Mary had worked in Okoyong. But already there was a change among the heathen people. The Gospel of Jesus has a wonderful power to change hearts and lives. As soon as word came that another worker was being sent to take her place, Mary got ready to leave for England.

At last the day came that Miss Dunlop, the new worker, arrived. Mary was ready to leave. Her friends carried her trunk and suitcases down to the Ekenge landing. A great crowd had come to the landing to tell her good-by and wish her a safe journey. Mary was telling them to help Miss Dunlop and to remain true to the Bible teaching. Suddenly a man was seen running through the crowd. He ran up to Mary.

"Come, white Ma, a young man has been shot in the hand, and he wants your medicine! "

"Don't go Ma, " said Ma Eme, Mary's friend. "You are tired and sick. You must get back to England. If you go with this man you may miss your boat. Let someone else go. "

"It is a bad tribe. They are always fighting. It is dangerous to go, " said Chief Edem. "Do not go with the man. "

"You cannot go, " said her other friends at Ekenge. "You are too sick to walk. The wild animals in the jungle will kill you. The wild warriors are out. They will kill you in the dark, not knowing who you are. "

"But I must go, " said Mary.

"If you must go, " said Chief Edem, "then you must take two armed men with you. You must get the chief of the next village to send his drummer with you. When the people hear the drum, they will know that a protected person is traveling who must not be hurt. "

It was night. Mary Slessor and the two men marched out into the darkness. The lanterns threw strange shadows that looked like fierce men in the darkness. At last Mary and her guard came to the village where they were to ask for the drummer. They told the chief what Chief Edem had said, but the chief did not want to help them.

"You are going to a fighting tribe, " said the chief. "They will not listen to what a woman says. You had better go back. I will not protect you. "

"You don't think a woman can do much. Maybe you are right, " said Mary to the chief. "But you forget what the woman's God can do. He can do anything. I shall go on. "

Mary went on into the darkness. The natives watched her go. She must be crazy, they thought. She had talked back to their chief who had the power to kill her. She had walked on into a jungle where wild leopards were ready to jump on her. She was going where men were drinking and making themselves wild. But Mary was not afraid. Once in talking about her trips through the jungle Mary said, "My great help and comfort was prayer. I did not used to believe the story of Daniel in the lions' den until I had to take some of those awful marches through the jungle. Then I knew it was true. Many times I walked alone, praying, 'O God of Daniel, shut their mouths! ' and He did. "

After pushing on through the darkness, Mary saw the dim outlines of the huts of the village. All was quiet. Suddenly she heard the swift patter of bare feet. She was surrounded by warriors shouting, pushing and shaking their spears.

"What have you come for? " asked the chief.

"I have heard a young man is hurt. I come to help him. I also heard that you are going to war. I have come to ask you not to fight, " said Mary.

The chief talked with some of his men. Then he came up to Mary.

"The white Ma is welcome, " he said. "She shall hear all we have to say before we fight. All the same we shall fight. Here is my son wounded by the enemy. We must wipe out the shame put on us. We must get even for this bad thing. Now Ma you may give my son your medicine. Then you must rest. Women, you take care of the white Ma. We will call her at cockcrow when we start. "

Mary fixed the young man's hand. Then she laid down in one of the huts for an hour's sleep. It seemed as though her eyes were hardly shut, before she heard a voice calling her.

"Ma, they are going to battle. Run, Ma, run! "

The warriors were on the warpath. Mary could hear their wild yells and the roll of the war drums. Mary ran after them. She was tired from the hard trip to their village. She was weak from the sickness she had. But nothing could stop her. She caught up with the warriors just as they were getting ready to attack an enemy village.

"Behave like men, " she yelled, "not like fools. Be quiet now. Do not yell and shout. "

The warriors became silent.

"God says that revenge is wrong, " said Mary. "He will pay back wicked people for the wrong things they do. You should not try to get even. Leave that to God. "

"No, no, " said the chief. "If we do not pay back for the wrong done us, the tribe will not be afraid of us. They will do more bad things to us. "

"Yes, yes, " shouted the warriors. They kept shouting and shaking their swords and guns.

"Did the whole village hurt you? Did the whole village shoot the young man? When you fight against the village you will hurt many women and children. They are innocent. They have done nothing. Let us pray to God about it. "

All the warriors were quiet as Mary prayed. She asked God to please stop the war if it was His will. She prayed for the young man who had been hurt. She prayed for whoever it was that hurt him, that he might turn away from his wickedness and become a Christian. She prayed for the people of the village.

Then Mary spoke to the warriors.

"You stay here, " she said, "I am going over to the village. "

Fearlessly she walked over to where the line of village warriors were drawn up with their swords and spears.

"Hello, " said Mary.

The warriors said nothing. Mary looked over the angry faces. Then she laughed.

"Nice bunch, " she said. "Is this the way you welcome lady visitors?"

The warriors stirred uneasily. They did not say anything.

"Where is your chief? " asked Mary. "Surely he is not afraid to talk to me. "

An old chief stepped out from behind the village warriors. To Mary's surprise he kneeled down in front of her.

"Ma, " he said, "we thank you for coming. It is true we shot the young man, the young chief of those who have come to fight us. But it was one man who did it. The whole village was not at fault. Please make peace. Tell us what we must do. "

Mary looked into the face of the chief. It was Chief Okurike. Long ago she had made a hard trip through the jungle in pouring rain to help when he was deathly sick. Because of what she had done then, he was now at her feet asking her to make peace. Mary shook hands with Chief Okurike. Then she spoke to his warriors.

"Stay where you are, " she said. "Some of you find a place where I can sit in comfort. I am hungry. Bring me breakfast. I will not starve while men fight. "

The warriors did as she told them.

"Now, " she said, "choose two or three men to speak for you. We shall have a palaver. In that way we will settle this thing. "

The four men met and talked with one another while Mary ate breakfast.

"Why do you want to fight and kill because one drunken man wounded your young chief? " Mary asked the men from the fighting tribe. "Let the tribe of the drunken youth pay a fine. "

A long talk followed. Sometimes it became very exciting. The arguing grew loud. The father of the young man wanted to have the man who had shot him punished hard. When the men became angry, Mary would stop them.

"Let us pray about this, " Mary would say. After she had prayed they would settle the point. Finally Mary and her God won out.

The fighting tribe at last agreed to be satisfied with a fine. The village paid the fine. They did not use money. So the fine was paid in barrels and bottles of trade gin. Now Mary was worried. What should she do? She knew the warriors would drink the gin right away. She knew this would make them fight after all in spite of their promises. A quick thought came to her. According to the law of these people, clothes thrown over anything gave it the protection of your body. No one else could touch it. Mary snatched off her skirt. She took off all the clothes she could spare. She spread them over the barrels and bottles. Now no one could touch them.

Mary took the one glass the tribe had. She gave one glassful to each chief to show that there was no trick and that the barrels and bottles were really filled with gin. Then she spoke to them about fighting. "If all of you go to your homes and don't fight, " said Mary, "I'll promise to send the stuff after you. I must go away. I have been sick and I must go where I can get strong again. I am going across the great waters to my home. I shall be away many moons. Will you promise me that you will not fight while I am gone? It will make me very happy if you will make that promise. It will make me sad if you don't, for I will always be wondering whether you are fighting and hurting one another. "

"I will promise, " said the chief of the village, "if the other chief will."

All the warriors looked at the chief whose son had been hurt. For a long time he said nothing. His tribe had always been fighters. It would be hard for them to give up fighting. The chief rubbed his chin. He scratched his head.

"Yes, Ma, " he said finally, "I will promise that we will not fight while you are gone. " The two villages kept the promise made by their chiefs. When Mary came back the two chiefs could say, "It is peace. "

Mary was very tired. Slowly she tramped through the hot jungle. After many hours she came to Ekenge.

"We have sent your trunks and things on ahead, " said Chief Edem. "Here are my best rowers and best soldiers. They are ready to take you to Duke Town. "

Mary once more stepped into the canoe. This time there was no one to call her back. Little black Janie, whom Mary had adopted, was with her.

"Good-by, good-by, Ma, " shouted the crowd. "God keep you safe and bring you back to us again. "

The rowers pulled their oars strongly, and swiftly down the slow moving river went the canoe. Three years Mary had spent in Okoyong. Already she had seen a change in the heathen people. A greater change was still to come. Mary was going to see more of the power the Gospel has to change heathen hearts and lives.

10

A Disappointment

Mary wrote to the Mission Board;

Charles and I are very much in love. We would like to be married. Charles is a wonderful Christian and a very fine teacher. He would be a very great help in my jungle work. We hope that you will agree to our marriage and let Charles go into the jungle with me.

I am ready to do what you say. I lay the whole matter in God's hands and will take from Him what He sees best for His work in Okoyong. My life was laid on the altar for that people long ago, and I would not take one jot or tittle of it back. If it be for His glory and the advantage of His cause there to let another join in it, I will be grateful. If not, I will be grateful anyway, for God knows best.

The Board was very much surprised to get this letter. If the Board members had thought about it at all, they had thought that Mary would never marry. She was forty-three years old and Charles Morrison, her sweetheart, was twenty-five. He was a mission teacher at Duke Town. The difference in their ages did not bother the sweethearts. They met and had fallen in love. They wanted to marry.

"I will marry you if the Mission Board will agree to letting you work in the jungle with me, " said Mary.

"But suppose the Board will not let me go into the jungle, wouldn't you be willing to come back to Duke Town with me? " asked Charles.

"No, Charles, I couldn't. I love you very much, more than anyone I have ever known, but my work for God is in the jungles. There no one else has yet planted the Gospel seed. To leave a field like Okoyong without a worker and go to one like Duke Town with ten or a dozen workers where the people have the Bible and plenty of privileges—that's foolish. If God does not send you into the jungle with me, then you must do your work and I must do mine where we have been placed. "

It was not long after Mary had returned to England that the Mission Board gave its answer to her request. The answer was no.

"What the Lord decides is right, " said Mary. "I believe that the Mission Board is giving me God's answer because they are His servants. "

What Mary suffered no one knew. She longed to have a life's partner by her side in the great work of bringing the Gospel to the jungle, but having given her life to God, she felt that He must be her first love. Charles Morrison, however, took the refusal very hard. He became sick and had to go home. Later he went to America where he died.

Now that Mary was home in England, she soon got over the jungle fevers. People wanted to hear about the missionary work in Africa. Mary went from church to church telling about her work. She did not like to do this. She would rather be in the jungle telling the natives about Jesus.

"It is hard for me to speak, " said Mary, "but Jesus has asked me to do it, and it is an honor to speak for Him. I wish to do it cheerfully. "

Everywhere people were thrilled to hear about the work for Jesus in the jungle. They wanted to do something, too. They gave money. They sent boxes of clothes and food and other things out to Africa to help the heathen.

Then Mary got sick with influenza and bronchitis. She could not go around speaking any more. Instead, she wrote some articles for a missionary paper.

"The Gospel must be preached to the people of Calabar, " she said. "Then the people ought to be taught some trades. They should learn to be carpenters and farmers and the like. We ought to send out people who can teach them these trades so that they can make a living. "

This was a new idea to many people. They wrote to other missionaries to find out what they thought about it. Later a school, "The Hope Waddell Training Institute, " was started. This school taught the boys and girls of Calabar many trades.

Mary was slow in getting well. She and Janie, the black girl she had brought with her, went to the southern part of England, where the climate was milder. It was hoped that the sea breezes and the mild climate would bring back her health. Days and weeks went by. Little by little Mary got better. The year 1891 came to an end. The bells rang in the New Year.

"Soon we can go back to dear Calabar, " said Mary. "Oh, how I want to get back and tell more people there about the Lord Jesus. "

In February, 1892, Mary and Janie sailed for Calabar. What new adventures awaited them in Africa?

"Welcome home, Ma, welcome, " shouted the people of Okoyong. "God bless you. Praise the Lord for sending you back to us! "

When Mary came back to Okoyong, things were much different from what they had been the first time she came. Now there was a fine mission house. Churches and schoolhouses had been built in many of the villages. The people were slowly but surely turning away from their heathen customs. Formerly no chief ever died without the sacrifice of many human lives, but this was not done any more. One of the chiefs said, "Ma, you white people are God Almighty. No other power could have done this. "

There were still many chiefs who liked to go to war and to fight with other tribes. But Mary had friends who would tell her of the plans of these chiefs. She would have to go to them and persuade them not to fight. One of Mary's dearest friends was Ma Eme. When she would hear of trouble, she would send a messenger to Mary with a medicine bottle. This would mean, "Be ready for trouble. "

Mary was so good at settling the arguments between the chiefs that the British government made her a vice-consul. This was something like a governor and judge. The jungle people would not let the white men come and make new laws or settle their arguments, but they did listen to Mary. She was a very fair and honest judge. The people loved and obeyed her.

But life was not easy. Not all the natives were Christians. Even those who were, were not always good Christians but would sometimes slip back into the old heathen ways. Then it was hard for Mary and her helpers to get to the different places. There were no easy roads through the jungles, and wild animals were always there ready to kill the careless traveler.

Mary received many gifts both from the natives and from her friends in England and Scotland. One of the gifts she loved the best was a little steamboat, which the natives called "smoking canoe. " The boys and girls in Scotland had given the money to buy this boat.

But Mary was not satisfied. She did not want to take life easy. As soon as she had built a church and the people were beginning to become civilized, she wanted to move on to wilder places.

"I want to start new work, " said Mary. "Let those who are younger and who have not been in this work as long as I have, take the places where the work has been begun. "

Many of Mary's friends among the natives had gone to Akpap, which was a village south of Ekenge. This village was about six miles from the Cross River. It was a large trading center. Many heathen came to this village to trade their goods for other things they wanted. Mary wrote to the Mission Board and asked them to let her begin work in this new place.

"We cannot at this time let you start work at Akpap, " wrote the Mission Board. "To start there we would have to build a mission house, and we do not have the money for that. Besides the nearest landing place is Ikunetu. This is six miles from Akpap. The forests are wild and hard to get through. We believe you should continue the work at Ekenge. "

Mary wrote again and again, trying to persuade the Board to let her start work at Akpap. At last the Mission Board agreed to let her start work there. They promised to build a mission house and a boathouse for her steamboat.

Mary did not wait for the house to be built. In 1896 she built a two-room native shed. Here she began her work. The house was not as good as the first house she built in Ekenge. This did not bother Mary. She was more concerned about bringing the Gospel to the heathen.

The work here was like that in Ekenge. The chiefs came with the troubles they were having in their tribes. They wanted her advice. The people came with their family problems and wanted her to tell them what to do. There were many heathen people who came from the jungle to visit her. Mary taught her classes. She conducted Sunday services. She was busy all the time. Then one day the smallpox sickness broke out.

"You must all be vaccinated, " said Mary to the natives. "I will scratch your arm with this medicine and the smallpox will stay away from you. "

Hour after hour, far into the night, day after day, Mary vaccinated the natives. When her medicine ran out, she took blood from the arms of those who had been vaccinated to use as vaccination medicine.

One day a man came running to the house where Mary was living in Akpap. He had run a long way. He was scratched up and sweating. He had run through the jungle without stopping.

"Ma, Ma, " he cried, "the smallpox sickness has come to Ekenge. Chief Ekponyong and Chief Edem are sick and many, many more. Come quick, oh, come to Ekenge or we shall all die. "

"I will come with you at once, " said Mary to the messenger from Ekenge. "I will help your people fight the smallpox sickness. "

Mary went back to Ekenge. The smallpox sickness was very bad. Nearly the whole village was sick.

"We must have a hospital, " said Mary. "I know what we will do. We will make my house here a hospital. "

Soon the house was filled to overflowing with sick people. She had to be doctor, nurse, and undertaker. Many of her close friends died. Chief Ekponyong, who at first had worked against Mary and then had become her friend, died. Chief Edem, the chief of Ekenge, was very sick. The tired missionary did everything she could to save the old heathen's life. But one dark night he died.

Mary was all alone. Mary made a coffin for the chief. She put his body in it. Then she dug a grave. She dragged the coffin to the grave and buried it. Completely tired out she dragged herself back to Akpap.

Just at this time Mr. Ovens and another missionary came up from Duke Town. They came to Mary's hut at Akpap. All was still and quiet. Mr. Ovens looked at the other missionary.

"Something is wrong, " he said. He knocked loudly at the door. He knocked and knocked again. Finally Mary awoke and opened the door. The missionaries saw how tired and sick she looked.

"What is wrong? " asked Ovens.

Mary told them about the sickness at Ekenge. She told them of what she had done. "I don't see how you could have done that work alone, " said Mr. Ovens.

"Won't you go and bury the rest of the dead? " asked Mary. "I was just too tired to do it. "

"Yes, we will, " said Mr. Ovens. The two missionaries went to Ekenge. There they found the mission house filled with dead bodies. They buried these people and preached to those who were still living about the Saviour.

Mary was weak and sick, but she kept right on working. In one of her letters to a friend she tells about some of her work:

Four are at my feet listening. Five boys outside are getting a reading lesson from Janie. A man is lying on the ground who has run away from his master, and is staying with me for safety until I get him forgiven. An old chief is here with a girl who has a bad sore on her arm. A woman is begging me to help her get her husband to treat her better. Three people are here for vaccination.

Every evening she would have family worship. Mary sat on the mud floor in one of the shed rooms. In front of her in a half-circle were the many children she had adopted and was taking care of. Behind them were the baskets holding the twin babies she had recently rescued. The light from a little lamp shone on the bright faces. Mary read slowly from the Bible. Then she explained the Bible reading to the children and prayed. Then she sang a song in the native language. The tune was a Scottish melody and as she sang she kept time with a tamborine. If any of the children did not pay attention, Mary would lean forward and tap his head with the tamborine.

Mary did not get her strength back. She was not well. The mission committee at Calabar decided that even though they had no worker to take her place, she must go home on a vacation which was long overdue.

"But who will take care of the work at Akpap? " asked Mary.

"Mr. Ovens, the carpenter, who is building the mission house at Akpap, can do the work until we find someone to take your place, " answered the chairman of the committee.

"But what shall I do with my many black children? I don't want them to go back to heathen ways of living while I am gone. I don't like to ask the other mission workers to take care of them for me. "

"Don't worry, Mary. We will find places for them. "

Places were found for all the adopted children except the four black children whom she planned to take along with her. These were Janie, who was now sixteen years old, Mary was five, Alice three, and Maggie was only eighteen months old. Now Mary had to find ways of clothing the children. The rags they wore in the jungle would not do for the trip to Scotland. Mary took her trouble to the Lord, and He wonderfully answered her prayer. When she reached Duke Town, she found that a missionary box had just come, and it had just the things she needed.

Mary took her children on board the big ship. It was the biggest "canoe" that any of the children except Janie had ever seen.

"We're on our way to bonny Scotland, " said Mary.

11

Clouds and Sunshine

"The other missionaries at Calabar, " said Mary, "work as hard, if not harder, than I do. We need more workers to preach the Gospel of Jesus Christ for your lost black brothers and sisters. They have souls just as you do. Jesus loves them just as He does you. We must tell them of His love. I would like to go farther inland to people who have never heard the Gospel and make a home among the cannibals."

Mary was giving a talk at one of the churches. As soon as she was well enough to make speeches, many of the churches wanted to hear her. The people were very much interested in the black children she had adopted and brought with her. Many of them had never seen black people before. Mary had some trouble speaking in English. For many years now she had been speaking almost all the time in the African language. It was sometimes hard for her to say the right English words, but the Holy Spirit helped her, and the people remembered her talks and gave generously for the work in Africa..

Late in the year 1898 Mary and the black children got on the big "canoe" and sailed back to Africa. They spent a happy Christmas on the ship.

Once more strong and well, Mary went back to work in Akpap. She taught the children and grownups. She healed the sick. She visited in the bush and in the jungle. During this time Mary had the joy of seeing six young men become Christians. These young men she trained and sent to the neighboring villages as Gospel workers. She had hoped for more helpers, but was grateful that God had given her these. More and more of the jungle people heard about her. Bushmen traveled hundreds of miles to see the white Ma who told them about Jesus.

Mary used every chance she had to tell the Gospel to heathen who had never heard it. The stories the visiting people told about their lands and the inland tribes filled Mary with the desire to explore other parts of the country. Often in the mission boat or in a canoe she traveled to villages farther away. On one trip the canoe in which

Mary was riding was attacked by a hippopotamus. Mary thought her end had come. Nevertheless, she bravely fought off the animal, using metal cooking pots and pans as weapons.

In the southern part of Nigeria was a strong, wild tribe called the Aros. They were a proud but wicked people. They made war on peaceful tribes. They would steal people from peaceful villages and make them slaves. They prayed to the Devil, and they killed people as human sacrifices to please their idols. They were cannibals who ate people.

The government decided to make this tribe stop doing these bad things. A small band of soldiers was sent against this tribe to make them obey. This made Mary sad. She knew that sending soldiers to fight against these people would not change them. She knew that only the Gospel could change the black men's hearts. She wished she could go to this tribe with the Gospel of Jesus, but the government said no. The government officers feared there might be a tribal war which would even come to Okoyong. They decided that Mary would be safer in Creek Town than Akpap. Sadly Mary left her friends and spent three months in Creek Town.

Her Okoyong friends did not forget her. They came often to visit her and brought her gifts. They also brought their quarrels to her to settle. They called her their queen. Finally, Mary was allowed to go back to Akpap.

Three years went by. It was now fifteen years since Mary had first come to Okoyong. On the anniversary of the day that she came a celebration was held. Seven young men whom Mary had won for Christ were baptized. The Rev. W.T. Weir, a missionary from Creek Town, helped in organizing the first Okoyong Christian Church. The following Sunday the church was filled to overflowing. Mary presented eleven children for baptism. The Lord's Supper was served for the first time to natives and white workers who had accepted Christ as their Saviour. After songs had been sung and speeches made by others, Mary got up to speak.

"You must build a church large enough to take care of all who come to hear God's Word. Okoyong now looks to you who have accepted Christ as your Saviour and who have joined the church for proof of the power of the Gospel, more than it looks to me. I am very happy over all that has been done these past fifteen years, but it is God who did it. To Him belongs all the glory. Mission houses, schools, and a church have been built. Wicked heathen customs have been stopped. Chiefs have quit fighting, and women are much better off than they were when I came. Let us praise God for this and let us go on and do greater things. The Lord will help us and will bless our work. "

Mary was happy the way the work was going, but she was not satisfied. She wanted to go to other places.

"This cannibal land of deep darkness with woods of spooky mystery is like a magnet, " said Mary Slessor. "It draws me on and on. "

"Where is this country where you want to work? " asked Miss Wright, one of the teachers at the Girls' Institute at Calabar.

"It lies to the west of the Cross River. It stretches for miles and miles toward the Niger River. "

"Haven't any missionaries been there? "

"None have gone into the forest. Missionaries and traders have gone along the edge of it when they went up the Cross River. "

"What tribes live in this dark and mysterious country? " asked Miss Wright.

"The Ibo tribe lives in most of the country, but they are ruled by the Aros clan, " said Mary.

"Who are they? Tell me something about them, Mary. I know so little about the tribes, except those who come to Calabar or send their girls to our Institute. "

"The Aros clan are a wise but tricky people. They live in thirty villages near the district of Arochuku, where I would like to begin a mission. They are strong and rule the Ibo tribe because of their trade and religion. They trade slaves, which their religion furnishes. When they cannot get enough slaves that way, they raid Ibo villages and capture the people who live there and sell them. "

"You say their religion furnishes them with slaves? How is that possible? "

"The Ibo tribe and the Aros pray to the juju god. They believe the juju god lives in a tree. They think this tree is holy. Each village has its own god and sacred tree, but the main juju used to be about a mile from Arochuku. "

"But you haven't told me about the slaves, " interrupted Miss Wright.

"I am just coming to that, " said Mary. "This main juju, called the Long Juju, was reached by a winding road that goes through a dense jungle and leads at last to a lake. In the center of the lake is an island on which was the Long Juju. Here hundreds of people came to ask advice from the priests and to worship. When the people came here, the Aros clan had captured them. Then they were either sold as slaves, sacrificed to juju, or eaten by the tribe. "

"How terrible! "

"The Aros are tricky. One of their tricks, was to throw some of the people they captured into the water. The water at once turned red. The priests would tell the people that juju had eaten the men. The people believed it, but really the red was only coloring the priests had thrown into the river. "

"Is the juju still there? " asked Miss Wright.

"No. The British soldiers went over the Cross River. They had a battle with the natives and beat them. They captured Arochuku. Then they chopped down the Long Juju. But of course the natives still have their village jujus. They still do many wicked things. "

"And you want to work among those terrible people? "

"Yes, don't you think they have a great need for the Gospel? "

"Oh, they do! But I would not have the courage to work among them. "

"I have no courage, " said Mary, "except what God gives me. "

"Tell me, Mary, have you gone into that country at all? "

"I have made some short exploration trips. I told the traders to tell the chiefs that some day I would come to their country to live, but their only answer was, 'It is not safe. ' That is what the people told me when I wanted to go to Okoyong. I trust in my heavenly Father and I am not afraid of the cannibals no matter how fierce and cruel they may be. "

"But Mary, did you know that when a chief died recently, fifty or more people were eaten at the funeral ceremonies, and twenty-five others had their heads cut off and were buried with the chief? "

"Yes, I heard that. But things were almost as bad when I came to Okoyong. God blessed my work, and He can protect me in this strange new land of the cannibals. I do hope the Mission Board will let me go and work among the Aros and Ibos. "

The missionaries in Calabar wanted Mary to work at Ikorofiong and at Unwana, which were two towns farther up the Cross River from Akpap. But Mary did not think these were good places for her work. She wanted to be where she could reach the most people. She wanted to work at Arochuku, the chief city of Aros which was also near the Efik, Ibo and Ibibio tribes. She wanted to open her first station at Itu, which was on the mouth of Enyong creek, her second station at Arochuku and a third at Bende. The missionaries at Calabar did not agree, but they decided to wait until a worker could be found to take Mary's place at Akpap. Mary would not reave these people until they could be taken care of by Christian workers.

"Send a minister to take care of a station. I cannot build up a church the way a minister can, " said Mary.

It looked as though Mary would not get to go to the land of Aros. Then Miss Wright, the teacher from the Girls' Institute, asked to be sent to Akpap as an assistant. This request was sent to Scotland for the Board to approve. Mary now decided to start work at once. In January, 1903, with two boys, Esien and Efiiom, and a girl, Mana, whom she had carefully trained, she loaded her canoe with food and other supplies and set off for the land of the cruel cannibals.

They did not know how the people there would treat them, but they trusted in God to take care of them and help them in their work. Mary found a house for them.

"I am leaving you here, " said Mary to the three natives, "to begin a school and hold church services for the people of Itu. I must go back to Akpap but I will come again as soon as I can. "

But Mary had to stay at Akpap longer than she expected. At last she was able to come again to Itu and to visit the school and the church services.

"You have done wonderfully well, " she told the three workers. "God has blessed your work. My heart was filled with joy when I saw so many people, young and old, at the services. And your school is filled with people who want to learn book and learn the will of God. Now we must build a church and a schoolhouse. "

Mary began mixing the mud and doing the other work that was necessary for building a building in Africa. The native workers and the people of Itu helped her gladly. It did not take long with many willing hands to build a church and school. Two rooms were added to the church building.

"These two rooms are for you, Ma, " the people said. "You must have a place to stay when you come to us. "

After the church and school were built, Mary went back to Akpap. Here she heard good news.

"The Board in Scotland has given me permission to be your assistant at Akpap, " said Miss Wright.

"Wonderful! " said Mary. "Now I can spend more time at Itu and more time in the jungle. "

On a beautiful morning in June, 1903, Mary packed her clothes and supplies and marched the six miles down to the landing beach at Ikunetu. Here she waited for the government boat which would take her to Itu. She waited and waited. At last she found one of the natives and asked, "Where is the government boat? Is it late? "

"No, Ma, it long time gone. "

So Mary had to walk back six miles through the jungle to the mission house at Akpap.

"Why, Mary, " said Miss Wright, "what are you doing here? I thought that by this time you would be traveling on the government boat to Itu. "

"I am in God's hands, " said Mary, "and He did not mean for me to travel today. I have been kept back for some good purpose. "

The next week when she again made the trip to board the boat, Colonel Montanaro who commanded the government soldiers in that part of the country, was on the boat.

"I will be happy to have you travel with me and my soldiers, " said the colonel. "You will be safer that way. I am going to Arochuku. "

"That is just what I would like to do, " said Mary. "Now I see why God did not let me travel last week. I have been wanting for a long time to visit the chief city of the Aros. I want to see more about this juju religion. "

Some time before, the government had sent soldiers into the country to make the chiefs stop the juju worship. The chiefs had promised to stop it, but it still went on secretly. After reaching Arochuku, Mary followed the jungle paths over which the slaves had been made to walk for hundreds of years. She came to the place of the Long Juju. There Mary saw the human skulls, the bones and the pots in which the bodies had been cooked. Mary shivered when she thought of the cannibal feasts.

Mary thought the people might be against her, but instead they welcomed her. They had heard about the good things she had done in the jungle.

"O God, " prayed Mary, "I want to bring the Gospel to these man-eaters for whom Christ died. Please, dear God, make the home church and the Mission Board see the great need here so that they will let me win this part of the country for Christ. "

Mary promised the people of Arochuku she would come again and open a school. Then she returned to Akpap and wrote the Mission Board for permission to open a station at Arochuku. Soon the answer came back!

We are sorry, but it will be impossible at this time to open work at Arochuku. We do not have the money or the workers.

12

Among the Cannibals

"The mission Board says that they cannot open a mission station at Arochuku now, " said Mary. "I have asked God to give me a mission station where His Gospel can be preached to the Aros. I trust in Christ who is able to do more than I am able to ask or think. I know God will give me what I have asked. "

"What are you going to do now? " asked Miss Wright.

"I am going to do what I believe God wants me to do. I am going to take some native Christians and make a beginning in the land of the Aros. "

Mary took some native boys whom she had trained. They were able to help with school-work and church services. Mary and the boys went to Amasu, a little village which was nearer the creek than Arochuku. Here she opened a school. It was soon filled with boys and girls thirsty for book and the loving God. She held church services for the people, and many of them came to hear the white Ma teach about Jesus.

At last it was time for Mary to go back to Akpap. She left the native Christians to carry on the work of the school and church. The people of the village gathered around her. They said,

"Come again soon, white Ma. If you do not care for us, who will care for us? "

As Mary went down the river in her canoe, she thanked God that He had let her open this new field to the Gospel. Suddenly there was a canoe barring her way. In it was a tall native.

"I have been waiting for you. My master at Akani Obio sent me to stop you and bring you to his house. "

Mary told her rowers to follow the native to his master's place. Soon they came to a trading place. Here Mary was greeted by a handsome young man.

"I am Onoyom Iya Nya, the president of the court and the chief of this district. This is my wife. Won't you please honor us by coming into our house? "

Onoyom and his wife led Mary to a European-type house, which was very nicely furnished. Onoyom's wife invited Mary to have some food with them. While they ate, Onoyom talked.

"Many times I have sent my servants to find you, " said Onoyom, "but they never found you until today. I am happy that you have come. "

"But why did you seek me? Why did you want me to come to you? " asked Mary.

"When I was a boy, " said Onoyom, "I served as a guide to a missionary. He told me the Gospel story. I wanted Jesus for my Saviour. But my tribe beat me and punished me in other ways until I gave up the white man's religion and followed the juju religion of the tribe. I took part in Arochuku feasts where we ate 'long pig, ' that is, men and women. "

"But why do you want to talk to me? " asked Mary.

"I never forgot what the missionary told me about Christ. Later I had troubles and sickness. I tried witchcraft to find the person who placed the troubles and sickness on me. Instead, I met a white man. He said to me, 'How do you know it is not the God of the white man who is angry with you? He is all-powerful. ' I said, 'How can I find this God? ' I hoped he would tell me, but he said, 'I am not worthy to tell you. Find the white Ma who goes to Itu and she will tell you. ' O Ma, please tell us about your God. "

Tears of joy ran down Mary's cheeks. Onoyom called all the members of his family and the servants together. Mary told them of Jesus and His power to save them. She read from the Bible, prayed with the people, and promised to come back again on her next trip.

"I will build a church for you, " said Chief Onoyom. "I have money. I will give $1,500 for a mission house and school. "

As Mary rode down the Enyong creek she thought of the new missionary work that was opening up.

"O God, " she prayed, "I thank You for the new places at Itu and Amasu. I thank You for the chance to build a church at Akani Obio. Please let me open a station soon at Arochuku. There with Your blessing I hope to conquer the cannibals for Christ. "

"I do hope, " she said to herself, "that the Board will soon send an ordained minister to take over the Akpap station. I must persuade Miss Wright to go with me to Itu. I am sure God will give her courage to come with me. This Enyong creek region will give us all the work for Christ we can handle and more. We must go forward for Christ. "

Mary made many trips to Akpap, to Itu and Amasu. She stopped at many little villages and lonely huts along Enyong creek to tell the people about the Saviour who had died also for those with black skins. Often she slept on mud floors. She ate yams and native fruits.

God blessed the work at Itu and Amasu. The people of Itu built a church and more than three hundred of them attended the services. At Amasu the school pew fast. The natives were learning to read.

The natives at Itu started to build a six-room house at Itu for Mary. It was to be one of the finest homes in which the missionary had ever lived.

"I am afraid it is too much work for you, " said Mary to the natives. "It is too big. " "No, it is not too much. " said the people of Itu. "Nothing is too much to do for you. We shall do it. "

Another time a native woman knelt at Mary's feet. She washed Mary's tired feet in warm water.

"You are so kind to me, " said Mary thanking her.

"I have been so afraid, Ma, that you would think us unworthy of a teacher and take her away, " said the woman. "I could not live again in darkness. I pray all the time. I lay my basket down and pray on the road. "

"That is good, " said Mary. "Prayer can do anything. I know. I have tested it. Of course, God does not always answer our prayers the way we want them answered, but He does answer them and in the way that is best for us. Trust God always. "

One day Mary thought of a new plan she wanted to try out. She had been in the jungle for five years. She was due to get a year's vacation at home in Scotland. Instead of this she asked for something else. She wrote to the Mission Board:

I would like to have leave from the mission station at Akpap for six months. This time I would spend traveling between Okoyong and Amasu. I would visit many places which I do not have time to visit now. Already I have seen a church and a mission house built at Itu, and a school and a couple of rooms at Amasu. I have visited several towns at Enyong and have found good enough places to stay.

I shall find my own canoe and crew. I shall stay at any one place just as long as I think wise. The members of my family [she meant the twins and slave children and other unwanted children she had adopted] shall help in teaching the beginners in the schools.

I plan to live at Itu as my headquarters. I will look after the small schools I have started at Idot and Eki. I will visit and work for Jesus in the towns on both sides of Enyong creek all the way to Amasu. I will live there for a while or travel among the Aros telling them of Jesus. Then I will come back by easy stages to Itu and home.

Please send an assistant to help Miss Wright at Akpap, so I will be free to do this new work in the jungle. I would like Miss Wright to help me with some work among the cannibals, in some places, so that I will have more time for pioneer work in the places farther away.

Itu should be our main station. We can reach the various tribes best from it. It is the gateway to the Aros and the Ibibios and near many other tribes. That is why it became a slave market. It could be reached so easily. It is only a day's journey from the seaport of the ocean steamers, having waterway all the year round and a good beach front. Itu is a natural place for our upriver and downriver work to come together.

Mary was now fifty-six years old. She had suffered much from sickness and from the lack of many things. Now she wanted to go on a "gypsying tour of the jungle, " as she called it. This was hard and difficult work. There were many dangers from wild animals and wild people. These tribes she wanted to visit did not know anything about the Saviour, or God's Word, but they did know how to do many wicked things like killing and eating people. Many a younger and stronger person than Mary would be afraid to tackle the job she had planned to do. Mary was not afraid. God had given her the chance to reach the wild cannibals. She was willing to die trying to bring the Gospel to them.

"I am willing to go anywhere, " said Mary, "provided it be forward among the cannibals. "

Mary anxiously waited for the answer from the Mission Board giving her permission to work for six months in the cannibal country. The answer did not come and did not come. At last she decided to go on a short trip through that country to encourage the black workers she had sent there. She went to see the Wilkies and Miss Wright.

"I am going on a short trip through the cannibal country, " said Mary. "I am inviting you to be my guests on this trip. I want you to see what God is doing among the cannibals. Won't you come with me? "

"We'll be glad to go with you, " said Mr. Wilkie.

Mary and her friends first visited Itu, where they met Colonel Montanaro, who had first taken Mary to Itu. Then they went to Akani Obio. Here Chief Onoyom had a big party for them.

"Ma, when are you going to come and stay a long time with us? " he asked. "I want you to bring the Gospel to me and to my people. "

"I hope it will be soon, " said Mary. "I am praying every day that the Mission Board will let me work in your country. "

Mary and her friends now went to Amasu to see the Gospel work that was being done there. Then they visited the villages around Arochuku where the Long Juju was. Then they started back to

Akpap. They visited many very small villages on the way back. Everywhere the people said to them, "We want to learn book. " They meant they wanted someone to teach them to read the Bible.

At last they arrived at Akpap. Here there was the letter from the Mission Board. Mary's hands shook as she opened the long-awaited letter. Would it give her permission to go to cannibal land or would it tell her to come home and take her furlough in the usual way?

You may make the jungle trip that you plan, but you will have to pay your own expenses during this time. We do not have any money for that work.

Mary was happy. Mary took the little money she had and bought supplies at Duke Town. Then she got her canoe ready. She took a crew of black rowers to row the canoe and a group of the black children she had adopted.

"It seems strange to be starting with a family on a gypsy life in a canoe, " wrote Mary, "but God will take care of us. Whether I shall find His place for me upriver or whether I shall come back to my own people again, I do not know. He knows and that is enough. "

At last Mary and her group of travelers came to Itu, which was deep in cannibal land. Mary had started the work here and then left native workers to carry on. Now there were three hundred people in the church. Mary found that the mission house at Itu was not finished. Mary herself mixed the cement for the floor while Janie did the whitewashing. Someone asked Mary how she learned to make cement.

"I just stir it like oatmeal, then turn it out smooth with a stick and all the time I keep praying, 'Lord, here's the cement. If it is to Your glory, set it, ' and it has never gone wrong. "

Every day Mary made calls and helped to solve the problems of the people of Itu. In the evenings she would hold prayer in the yards of many of the people. Always Mary told the people of the Saviour who died for them.

The news that Mary the white Ma was in cannibal land soon spread far and wide. The tom-toms calling through the jungle told the different tribes where Mary was. From Ibibio southward, the natives sent messages to Mary.

"Please, Ma, " they said, "send us a teacher. "

"It is not 'book' I want, " said a chief in his message, "I want God. "

"We have three in hand for a teacher, " said Chief Onoyom of Akani Obio. "Some of the boys have already finished the books Mr. Wilkie gave us. We can do no more until you send us help. "

Mary spent the night praying to God to send more workers to Africa. "O Britain, " said Mary, "filled full of ministers and church workers, but tired of Sunday and of church, I wish that you could send over to us what you are throwing away! "

13

Blessings Unnumbered

God blessed Mary's work in cannibal land and more and more people were won for Jesus. Chief Onoyom stayed true to his faith.

"Come, " he said to his people, "we must build a church here at Akani Obio. Let us go to the jungle and cut down trees for the house of God. "

Chief Onoyom and his people went to the woods. The chief went to a tree and got ready to cut it down.

"Chief, " they cried, "you are not going to cut that tree, are you? You know that is the juju tree. "

"I know it is the juju tree, " said Onoyom, "and I am going to chop it down. "

"The juju will be angry. He will not let us. He will kill us, " cried the people.

"Ma's God is stronger than our juju, " said Chief Onoyom. "Cut it down. "

The people began to chop. The trunk of the tree was thick. After a while they stopped.

"See, we cannot cut it, " they said.

The heathen natives were glad.

"Aha, " they said, "our juju is stronger than Ma's God. "

The next morning Chief Onoyom took some men who wanted to be Christians. Before beginning to chop at the tree they knelt and prayed that the white Ma's God would prove stronger than the juju. Then they got up and began to chop. Soon the tree fell with a mighty crash. Ma's God had won!

The juju tree was used for a pulpit and seats in the church building. A large group of people came to the dedication services. They were quiet and well-behaved. What a great change the Gospel had made! Only two years before the people were wild savages.

Mary had to hold services at Arochuku out-doors, but now the people built a church and a schoolhouse. At other villages along Enyong creek congregations were organized, and churches and schoolhouses were built.

In 1905 Mary had to go to the Mission Council meeting at Calabar. During the meeting Mary was called on to tell about her work.

"God has done great things in cannibal land. We have congregations at Itu, Arochuku, Oko, Akani Obio, Odot, Amasu, and Asang. In all of these places churches have been built. In many of them we have built schoolhouses too. Many of the cannibals are being won for Christ. But we need more workers. In all this wide country of the Aros, I am the only white missionary. My six months' leave is almost up. Who will take care of these people who are as dear to God as you or I? Now they are being taken care of by native workers, but these have only little training. Send workers to cannibal land to change these man-eaters into Christians. "

The Council was thrilled by Mary's report. They voted that she could spend six more months in cannibal land, but again they said she would have to pay her own expenses. This did not bother Mary. She had never been paid, much salary. In the first years she sent most of it back home to take care of her mother and sister. After they had died she used me most of it for her colored Christians. She had adopted many black children whose parents had thrown them out. But money never bothered Mary. She had a little bit saved up. She was happy that she could go to cannibal, land and win souls for Christ.

"But where shall I work now? " Mary asked herself. "Shall I keep on working on upper Enyong creek or shall I go south to the Ibibios? The Ibibios are the worst heathen in this part of Africa. The worse the people are, the more they need help. I should go to the Ibibios. "

Meanwhile the Mission committee in Scotland decided to build a hospital at Itu. Dr. Robertson was to be the head of it. The Mission committee chose a name for the hospital. They named it, "The Mary Slessor Mission Hospital. " The people in Scotland gave the money so the hospital could be built.

"It seems like a fairy tale, " said Mary when she was told about it, "and I don't know just what to say. I can just look up into the blue sky and say, 'Even so, Father; let me live and be worthy of it all. ' It is a grand gift and I am so glad for my people. "

Now that Itu was taken care of, Mary had all the more reason to go south to the Ibibios. In their country the government was building roads and setting up courts. The government people wanted Mary to come to that country too, because she knew so much more about the people and customs in cannibal land.

"Get a bicycle, Ma, " said one of the government men. "Here is the road. Come as far as you can. And we'll soon have a motorcar for you. "

Mary started out. She took along one of the boys she had adopted. It was twelve-year-old Etim. He could read and she needed his help. Once more Mary was beginning mission work in a new part of the country where Christians had never been.

Mary and Etim went to Ibibio-land. Mary started a school and a small congregation. Etim was made the teacher of the school. He proved to be a very good teacher. Soon he had a class of fifty children.

"It is my hope, " said Mary, "that Ikotobong will be the first of a chain of stations stretching across the country. "

Mary went to visit the old chief of Ikotobong.

"What do you think of our work here? "

"It is good, " said the chief. "I am happy you came. There are many things that are strange to me and my people. We do not understand them. I am glad for the light. We will give Etim food as pay for teaching. We will help build a schoolhouse and a church. "

Mary was happy that the people were willing and anxious to learn. But she wanted to go to a new part of the country and start more places. The government officer at Ikot Expene gave Mary a bicycle.

"I think it's God's will that I learn to ride this bicycle. Think of an old lady like me on a bicycle! " said Mary. "The new road makes it easy to ride, and I'm running up and down and taking a new work in a village two miles off. It has done me all the good in the world, and I will soon be able to do even more work. "

The treatment of the women in Ibibio was very bad. They were treated worse than slaves. The men could do whatever they wanted to do with them. They were often beaten. They were bought and sold like cattle. Mary wanted to help the poor women.

"I want to build a home for girls, orphans, twins and their mothers, and those who have run away from harems, " said Mary. "I also want to start a school where trades and skills can be taught. All the women know how to farm. They know how to weave baskets and make simple sandals. But I want them to know many more things so that they can take care of themselves. I am going to look for a place with good land and pure water near the roads and the markets. Then I will write to my friends and to the Mission Board for help. "

Mary's furlough had first been for six months and then was made six months longer. In April, 1906, it came to an end. She was supposed to go back to Akpap, because the Mission Council expected her to settle down in one place and work there. They appointed her to work at Akpap and that is where they expected her to work.

"I do not want to settle in one place, " said Mary. "God gives me different gifts; I think my gift is to explore and start new congregations. Others are better fitted to take care of them after they are started than I am. God is pushing me onward. I don't dare look backward. Even if my dear church turns against me and will not have me as its missionary, I must go forward. I can find food for myself and the children. That is all I need. God will help me. "

Mary thought and prayed much over this matter. She thought of starting a store or taking a government job so she could earn money to take care of the missionary work. She wrote a long letter to the

Mission Board. She told how God had blessed the work at Itu and the villages on Enyong creek. Then she wrote:

In all this how plainly God has been leading me. I did not think of doing these things in my lifetime, but God has led me on. First Itu, and then the Creek, then back from Aro, where I had set my heart, to a lonely, spooky, wilderness. There no one ever went, but now miles of roads are being built.

The Board says I am to go back to Akpap in April. I love no other place on earth so well. But I dare not think of leaving the crowds of untamed, unwashed, unlovely savages, and take away the little sunlight that has begun to flicker out over its darkness.

I know that I am pretty old for this kind of work. But God will help. Whether the church permits or not, I feel that I must stay here. I must even go farther as the roads are made. I cannot walk now and I must be careful of my health. But I can get four wheels made and set a box on them and the children can pull me. I dare not go back. If the Board insists, I will risk finding some other way to support myself and my family.

As April drew closer day by day, Mary anxiously waited for the Mission Board's answer. The Mission Board wrote to Mary:

We are sending John Rankin to look over the field where you have been working. After he has made his report we will decide what you should do.

Mr. Rankin visited the different places in cannibal land where Mary had started congregations. He talked with the chiefs and the people. One chief talking about Mary and the other women missionaries said, "Them women be the best men for the mission. " He wrote to the Board:

Close to Arochuku, within a circle of less than three miles in diameter, there are nineteen large towns. I visited sixteen of these. Each of them is larger than Creek Town. Most of the people are anxious to help. Already many of them have begun to live in God's way. Even the head chief of all the Aros wants us to do mission work in his country. He told the other chiefs he is going to rule according to God's way. He wants missionaries to be sent to his people. He offers to build a house at Arochuku for any missionary who will come.

The Mission Board was thrilled when they read this report. They agreed to give the money for the work which Mary had planned. They appointed Rankin to take charge of the stations at Itu and Arochuku. They agreed to let Mary go into the new territory. She did not have to go back to Akpap.

This made Mary very happy. Now she could work full time among the Ibibios. She offered to pay for the building of a mission station among the Ibibios if there was no money in the homeland treasury. In May the government appointed Mary to take charge of the courts in the Ibibio district as she had done in Okoyong. It paid her for this work so now she had money to carry on her mission work whether the Board paid her or not.

Court was held at Ikotobong. Three chiefs and a jury helped Mary in trying the cases, but Mary's word was law. Mary was fair and kind, but at the same time she saw to it that those who did bad things were punished. In a letter to a friend she wrote:

God help those poor helpless women. They are treated worse than animals. Today I had a crowd of people. How wicked they were! I have had a murder, a poison bean case, a suicide, a man branding his slave wife all over her face and body, a man with a gun who shot four people. It is all horrible.

But her work as judge did not stop her from doing her mission work. Everywhere she went she told the natives of Jesus' death for them. She opened schools and churches for natives. She also was thinking about the other missionaries. She planned a place for them where they could spend weekends or where they could rest when they were getting over sickness. She chose a place half-way between Itu and Ikotobong on Enyong Creek. It was high above the lowlands where most of the sickness was. A friend sent her a check for $100 and Mary used it as a start for this rest home. She had the ground cleared and a small English house built.

Although Mary was busy she was not well. During most of 1906 she had been ailing.

"If you want to keep on with your missionary work, " said the government doctor, "you must go home to Scotland where you can rest up and get the fever out of your system. "

Mary did not want to leave her work. A few days after her talk with the doctor, when he came to see her again, she was much better.

"It looks as if God wants me to stay. Does that sound like He could not do without me! I do not mean it so. How little I can do! But I can at least keep a door open for missionary work so others can come and do more. "

The year 1907 came. Mary was much worse. She could walk only a few steps. When she wanted to go anywhere, she had to be carried. At last she decided to do as the doctor told her and go to Scotland for a vacation.

"Oh, the dear homeland! " she said with tears in her eyes. "Shall I really be there and worship in the churches again? How I long for a look at a winter landscape, to feel the cold wind, and the frost in the cart ruts! How I want to take a back seat in a church and hear the congregation singing, without a care of my own! I want to hear how they preach and pray and rest their souls in the hush and silence of our home churches. "

Mary took her six-year-old Dan, one of the many children she had adopted. The government officers were kind and helpful to her in getting ready for her trip.

"God must repay these men, " said Mary, "because I cannot. He will not forget that they did it to a child of His, unworthy though she is. "

Mary was now a wrinkled, shining-eyed old lady, almost sixty years old. She was carried on board the ship that would take her to Scotland. Her friends, both white and native, cried and wondered if she would ever come back to Africa again.

14

Journey's End

"Send us workers for dark Africa, " said Mary. "If I can get the Board to send us one or more workers, I will give half my salary to add to theirs. I will give the house for them to live in and find the servants. You who have so much, won't you do something for these poor people of Africa? "

Mary was speaking in the churches of Scotland telling about her work in Africa. After she had returned to Scotland, she felt much better. The air and climate was much better than in the steaming jungles of Africa. As soon as she was strong enough, she began to go about telling about her work. She urged the people to give money and to send workers to Africa.

Above all, she wanted to get money to support the industrial home for women which she had planned. From May until October she went among the churches telling about the "African sheep" whom the Good Shepherd Jesus wanted brought in.

In October Mary asked to be sent back to Africa. She wanted to carry on her work there.

"I am foolish, I know, " said Mary, "but I just feel homeless without any relatives here in Scotland. I am a poor, lonesome soul with only memories. "

Back in Africa Mary was busier than ever, holding court, looking after her home, and doing missionary work. On Sundays she held a half-dozen or more services in the nearby villages in which lived the people with whom she worked during the week. On some of these trips she brought back orphan children to join her already "overstuffed" household. But all this work was too much for her. She became sick again and very weak. Now her eyes began to get weak, so that she could not see as well. But nothing could stop her. She started the building of the industrial home for women and girls. She planted fruit trees there and planned to raise rubber and cocoa and cattle.

Mary wanted to move again. Some natives had come from Ikpe to see her before she went on her vacation to Scotland. They asked her to bring the Gospel to them. Now they came again.

"We have heard of the great white Mother and we want to learn to be God's men, " they said.

Mary made a two-day canoe trip to their town. Ikpe was a large town with many people in it. But the people were very wicked. They did all the wicked heathen things that were against God's commandments. But there were people in it who wanted to become Christians. They had begun to build a small church building to which they had added two rooms for the missionary.

Mary held a service in the church. Many people had gathered to hear for the first time the news of how Jesus saves us. After the end of the service Mary decided that it was God's will for her to move to Ikpe. But she had to arrange for someone to take care of her other work first.

When she came home from this trip she was sick again. As soon as she was a little better she busied herself with the women's home. She wanted to get that running well before she left for Ikpe. The natives of Ikpe sent some more of their people to visit her and beg her to come to Ikpe. Whenever she could, she made trips to that village. Often she took other missionaries with her.

In November, 1909, she resigned from her court work. The government did not like to lose her because she knew so much about the natives and their customs. But the government knew that Mary's first love was her missionary work. They let her give up her court work and thanked her for all she had done.

"Just a few more things to take care of, " said Mary, "and I will be ready to start for Ikpe. Those faithful people deserve a worker. They are holding services even though they know very little of Christianity. I must go there. I know God wants it. "

It was the year 1910 and Mary was sure that now she could begin her work in the new territory that looked so promising. Suddenly Mary became very, very ill. The government sent its official automobile to take her to the Mary Slessor Hospital at Itu. Did God want Mary to work at Ikpe? Or would someone else preach the Gospel there?

For many weeks Mary lay sick in the hospital at Itu. At last she was much better.

"You must go to Duke Town for a longer rest, " said the doctor.

"But, Doctor, " said Mary, "I have my work to do, I cannot spend my time lying in bed. "

"If you are unwilling to rest at Duke Town, I shall have to send you to Scotland on a long vacation. "

"Very well, " sighed Mary, "I will go to Duke Town. "

The next day the government sent its boat, the "Maple Leaf, " to take Mary down the river to Duke Town. Here she spent many weeks resting and gaining her strength. At last the doctor agreed that she could go back to her work at Ikotobong. Once more the government sent its boat to take her back to her mission station.

"I want to go to Ikpe soon, " said Mary, "but first I want to establish a station at Ikot Expene and at other places along the way. "

Whenever she felt strong enough, she rode her bicycle through the jungle to Ikot Expene choosing places for schools and churches along the way, talking to chiefs, and getting the things ready for more places where the Gospel could be preached.

The people at Ikpe were holding services even though they knew very little about Christianity.

"Soon the white Ma will come, " they said. "She will tell us more about Jesus. "

A native teacher from another station, who had received training from Mary, taught the people what he knew about the Gospel.

"Oh, why cannot the church send two workers to Ikpe? " said Mary. "Why don't they use the money on hand for that? If there isn't enough money left after two years, let them take my salary. I shall be only too glad to live on native food with my children. "

Mary was busy collecting building materials and other things for the church of Ikpe. At last the time came. God wanted Mary at Ikpe. How happy Mary was! How happy were the faithful people at Ikpe who had waited so long!

Mary at once was busy with much work. She quieted mobs, she calmed quarreling chiefs, she held meetings with the crowds, and on Sundays conducted services. One day the smallpox broke out. The government sent down men to vaccinate the natives so the sickness would not spread. Mary heard shouting and yelling in the streets. She looked out of her house. The natives were yelling and shouting and waving guns and swords. Mary went up to the crowd.

"What is this? " asked Mary. The crowd kept yelling.

"Be quiet, " shouted Mary and held out her hands. "Let your chief speak. "

"Ma, " said the chief, "my people are afraid of the white man's juju. It makes the people sick. " He meant the vaccination.

"The vaccination may make a little sickness, but it keeps you from getting the big sickness, " said Mary. Then she told them how vaccination had helped other tribes. She showed them her vaccination. After a long talk with the chiefs and the people the matter was peaceably settled.

Mary wanted to keep in touch with her former headquarters at Ikotobong. She made many canoe trips back and forth. These trips were very hard on her and she did not rest well. Many people wondered how Mary could keep on working, but she trusted God who made her strong to carry on.

During 1911 a tornado struck Mary's house at Use, one of the stations. She fixed the house herself. During this she strained herself and had a heart attack which was followed by a severe fever. Sometimes the fever was so great she was delirious. But still she would not stop working. She continued to teach school and hold worship services on Sunday.

Dr. Hitchcock of the Slessor Hospital came to see her every week.

"You must not go to Ikpe again, " he said. "You must not ride your bicycle. You must spend more time resting. "

But Mary disobeyed the doctor and held services the following Sunday. It was too much for her. She almost fainted before the service was over.

"You must stay in bed, " said Dr. Hitchcock, "until you are well enough to get up. "

"All right, doctor, " said Mary.

"And you must eat meat twice a day, " said the doctor.

"But I'm not a meat-eater, " answered Mary.

"You're going to be, or I will send you to Duke Town for a long rest."

Mary laughed. "I've all my plans made and I must not draw a salary without doing something for it. "

At last the doctor sent her to the Slessor Hospital for a rest. Because of her hard work, she had a bad fever sickness. Now Mary saw that she was foolish in not listening to the doctor.

"Life is hardly worth living, " she said, "but I am doing what I can to help the doctor to help me, so I can be fit again for another spell of work. "

The Christians at Ikpe sent some men to see Mary to ask her when she would be back. "Seven weeks, " said Dr. Hitchcock.

"I may run up sooner than that, " said Mary. "I'm very well if the doctor would only believe it. "

Near the end of 1911 Mary was allowed to leave the hospital. She hurried to her friends at Ikpe. But Mary still was not very strong. Her friends in Calabar and in Scotland urged her to take a long-earned furlough. While thinking about this, Mary decided to have a box on wheels made so that she could get around since the doctor would not let her use her bicycle. Some friends heard about this and they sent her a light cart which could be wheeled by two boys or girls.

"Now I don't need a furlough, " said Mary. "Instead of going home as I had planned, I shall stay here and enjoy going over ground in my cart that I couldn't get over otherwise. "

A new government road was being built between Ikpe and Ikot Expene. Mary wanted to start schools and churches all along this road. But she was not strong enough to carry out her idea. Her heart was very weak now and she had to rest often. If there had been someone to take her place, she would have gone home for a rest. Mary wrote to a friend:

We were never so shorthanded, and I can do what others cannot, what indeed, doctors would not allow them to try. No one meddles with me and I slip along and do my work using less strength than many would have to use.

Mary knew if she took a furlough her work at Ikpe and the other stations would stop because there was no one to take her place. This she did not want to happen. She worked on through the summer of 1912. In September she completed thirty-six years as a missionary in Africa.

"I'm lame and feeble and foolish, " said Mary, "but I grip on well. "

Her friends were very much worried about her health. It was suggested that she be sent on an expense-paid trip to the Canary Islands. There the climate was milder than it would have been in Scotland during the winter. She was glad to go. Mary wrote:

What love is wrapped around me! It is simply wonderful. I can't say anything else. Oh, if I only get another day to work. I hope it will be fuller of earnestness and blessing than the past.

This vacation was a real blessing to Mary. The fevers left her. With no committee meetings, no court cases or other problems to worry about, she grew stronger very quickly. It was not many months before she was back at Duke Town. The doctor gave her an examination.

"You're as sound as an elephant's ivory tusk, " said the doctor. "You are good for many years, if you will only take care. "

Mary did not like that. She had never been willing to sit and twiddle her thumbs. Now her mind was full of new plans for more work. She wanted to get busy with her work for the Lord.

For the next two years Mary worked hard at Use and Ikpe. She traveled between these two places, sometimes in a canoe, sometimes in the government boat, but mostly in her two-wheeled cart. There was still much to do. She was still fighting the juju worship, the sinful practice of eating people and the murdering of twins.

Eight years had gone by since Mary had left Akpap. A new church was being finished and the missionaries who now worked there invited Mary to attend the dedication service. Mary wanted to see the dear friends she had loved for years. She decided to go and take her adopted children with her.

From all over Okoyong the people had come to see their Ma, their White Queen. Ma Eme, the missionary's old friend, was there. When they met tears filled their eyes, they were so happy to see one another again. But Mary was sad, too, because Ma Eme had never openly accepted Christianity. Speaking of Ma Eme, Mary said, "My dear and old friend and almost sister, she made the saving of life so often possible in the early days. It is sad that she would not come out for Christ. She could have been the honored leader of God's work. Hers is a foolish choice. And yet God cannot forget all she was to me and how she helped me in those dark and bloody days. "

Hundreds of people crowded into the new church at Akpap. Mary remembered the wild parties and drunken fights of the first days of her work among the people. How they were changed! How God had changed them through His Gospel! It was wonderful! Mary thanked God for His wonderful blessings.

Shortly after her trip to Akpap, Mary was honored by the king of Great Britain. She was chosen by him to be a member of the order of St. John of Jerusalem. This was an honor given only to English

Christians who had done great things for God. The government people of Calabar decided that they must have a public celebration of this great honor. They sent the government boat for Mary. The little old missionary, now nearly sixty-five, was brought to Duke Town. Here a great crowd filled the biggest hall in town.

The governor made a speech and pinned the cross on Mary's left shoulder. During the speech Mary sat with her head in her hands. When it came time for her to speak, she found it hard to talk. Turning to the boys and girls who were in the hall she said, "Be faithful to the government. Be Christians. Be friends of the mission and be followers of Jesus. "

Later she wrote to her friends in Scotland:

Don't think there is any change in me because I received this honor. I am Mary Slessor, nothing more and none other than the unworthy, unprofitable but most willing servant of the King of kings.

The only change the honor made in Mary was that she worked harder than ever. A government road was opened to Odoro Ikpe. Mary at once started a mission there and reached out into the small jungle settlements. There she talked with the chiefs and the natives. At last she won their consent to build schools and churches. They gave her the land to do this. Now she was beginning all over in a new territory. She had the same hard work, the same troubles, the same heathen customs to fight. But Mary was glad to do it. She thanked God for the chance to bring the Gospel to people who had never heard about it.

Mary saw to it that a house was built and then began teaching in the school, holding services, settling quarrels, winning souls for Jesus. In August, 1914, rumors reached her that Europe was rushing into war. This made her feel sick. She knew that this war would not only bring suffering, horror, and death to many of her dear friends, but it would also hinder the work in Calabar.

Several months went by. The mail came. Mary opened the newspaper. There she read the headlines: Russia declares war! France declares war! England declares war! Mary fainted. The trouble and excitement were too much for her. For two weeks more she carried on her work but it was too much for her. She became weaker and weaker. On Sunday, January 10, 1915, she held her usual church service. After the church meeting she fainted. Dr. Robertson arrived from the Slessor Hospital at Itu. He was able to bring her to, but on January 12 she found it almost impossible to talk. Her last words were a prayer in the African language called Efik.

"O Abasi, sana mi yok, " said Mary. "O God, release me! "

Janie, the first twin Mary had saved, was now a beautiful black woman. She and other children Mary had saved and adopted were watching beside Mary's bed through the night. A rooster crowed.

"Day must be dawning, " said one of the girls.

Day was dawning for Mary, God's eternal day. She slipped away from the earth to be with her Saviour in Heaven.

"Our Mother is dead, and we shall be slaves now that our Mother is dead, " cried the natives. The news that the white Ma was dead spread rapidly. Natives came from all over the country to see the woman they loved.

Mary's body was taken to Itu where services were held. Then it was taken to Duke Town. Here another service was held. Then the coffin was carried to the beautiful cemetery on Mission Hill. From this place could be seen a large part of the city where Mary had begun her faithful missionary work in Africa. Around her grave the grateful natives gathered and wept for her who had wept and prayed over them.

"Do not cry, do not cry, " said old Ma Fuller, Mary's native friend through the years. "Praise God for His blessings. Ma was a great blessing. "

First the Africans called her "the white Ma who lives alone. " Then they called her "the Ma who loves babies. " But lastly they called her "eka kpukpru owo, " "everybody's Mother. "

THE END

115

BOOKS ON WOMEN MISSIONARIES

* * * * *

WHITE QUEEN OF THE CANNIBALS

The Story of Mary Slessor By A. J. Bueltmann

When Mary was young, she heard her mother read about the dangers and rewards of missionary work in Calabar, Africa. This challenged Mary Slessor's young heart and she determined to serve her Lord there. *White Queen of the Cannibals* records her courage as a missionary to the worst of pagans. The story is simply told that it might inspire children to Christian service.

NOT ALONE By Eunice V. Pike

Many hundreds of languages in the world today have never been reduced to writing. Uncounted thousands of people cannot read God's Word. The work of Wycliffe Bible Translators is to master the language of a tribe, reduce it to writing, and then teach the people to read the Scriptures—in their own tongue. Eunice Pike recounts her years spent with the Mazatec Indians in Mexico, giving them God's Word.

CLIMBING By Rosalind Goforth

After returning home from many years of missionary service in China, Rosalind Goforth reflects on those incidents that most affected her life for Christ. Written to display the mercy of the Lord and "to help others face life's hard problems, " the author recalls her experiences from childhood to retirement—a life of constant *climbing*.

116

232765LV00004B/136/P

9 781409 937982